I LOVE ISLAM

3

CD Included

ISLAMIC STUDIES TEXTBOOK SERIES - LEVEL THREE

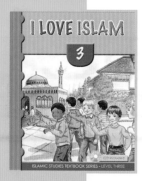

I Love Islam 3

بسم الله الرحمن الرحيم

In the Name of Allah, Most Compassionate, Most Merciful

I Love Islam © is a series of Islamic Studies text-books that gradually introduces Muslim students to the essentials of their faith. It brings to light the historic and cultural aspects of Islam. The series covers levels one through five, which are suitable for young learners. It includes student textbooks and workbooks, as well as teacher and parent guides.

The Islamic Services Foundation is undertaking this project in collaboration with Brighter Horizons Academy in Dallas, Texas. Extensive effort has been made to review the enclosed material. However, constructive suggestions and comments that would enrich the content of this work are welcomed.

All praise is due to Allah (God), for providing us with the resources that have enabled us to complete the first part of this series. This is an ongoing project, and it is our sincere wish and hope that it will impact our Muslim children today and for many years to come.

Copyright © 2016 by Islamic Services Foundation

ISBN 1-933301-22-8

PROGRAM DIRECTOR *
Nabil Sadoun, Ed.D.

WRITING TEAM
Narmeen Al-Omar
Nabil Sadoun, Ed.D.
Majida Yousef

REVIEWERS AND ADVISORS
Susan Douglass
Freda Shamma, Ph.D.

CONTRIBUTORS
Ummukulthum Al-Maawiy
Basma Asad
Lana Baghal Dasti
Nicholas Howard
Hayah Sharif
Menat Zihni

CURRICULUM DESIGN
Majida Salem
Nabil Sadoun, Ed.D.

ENGLISH EDITOR
Sumaiya Susan Gavell

GRAPHIC DESIGN
Mohammed Eid Mubarak

ILLUSTRATIONS
Raed Abdulwahid
Sujata Bausal
Ramendra Sarkar
Special thanks to: Goodword Books

ISLAMIC SONGS
Noor Saadeh,
NoorArt, Inc.

POEMS
My Two Angels: Khadijah Stephens,
Mosque of the Internet

PHOTOGRAPHY
Al-Anwar Designs
Isam Alimam

PUBLISHER AND OWNER

ISF PUBLICATIONS

Islamic Services Foundation
P.O. Box 451623
Garland, Texas 75045
U.S.A
Tel: +1 972-414-5090
Fax: +1 972-414-5640
www.myislamicbooks.com

Printed in the United States of America

UNIT A

ARKANUL-IMAN: PILLARS OF FAITH

UNIT B

FAITH IN ACTION: THE STORY OF PROPHET IBRAHEEM

WORSHIPPING ALLAH

PROPHET MUHAMMAD IN MAKKAH

UNIT E

ISLAM IS CHARACTER

I Love Islam: Friends and Family

Zaid   Leena   Mr. Mahmood   Mrs. Mahmood

Bilal   Sarah   Mr. Siraj   Mrs. Siraj

Amir   Omar   Mona   Khalid

Ahmad   Teacher Hibah   Baby Yousuf

-5·24

ARKANUL Iman: PILLARS OF FAITH

What Is Iman?

Q u e s t i o n s ?

❶ What does *iman* mean?
❷ Are Islam and iman the same?
❸ What are *arkanul-iman*?

Main Idea: *Iman*, or faith is the heart of Islam. We need to keep our iman strong so that our Islam will be complete. To do that, we should learn the pillars of iman very well.

Word
W a t c h

Arkan (Pillars)	أركان
Rukn (Pillar)	ركن
Iman (Faith)	إيمان
arkanul-iman	أركان الإيمان

Think about it!

What would happen to a tree without roots?

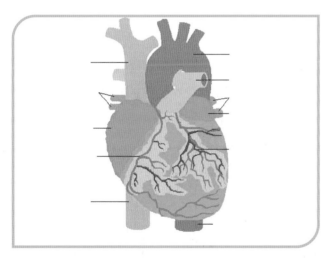

What would happen to a person without a heart?

What would happen to a building that has a weak foundation?

Zaid Learns About Iman

Zaid said to his father, "I know what Islam is and what the five pillars of Islam are. But what is *iman*?"

Father said: Let us review the five pillars of Islam first:

1. Shahadah (Testimony)
2. Salah (Prayer)
3. Zakah (Charity)
4. Siyam (Fasting)
5. Hajj (Pilgrimage)

Father: Zaid do you know what arkan or rukn mean?

Zaid: Arkan means pillars; rukn is one pillar? That is a column in a building, and it is really important because it holds the building together.

Father: Great, Zaid!

Zaid: But I still do not understand what iman is. Is it the same as Islam?

Father: Imagine that Islam is a tree, Zaid. Can a tree stand strong without deep strong roots?

Zaid: No. We learned in science that without roots a tree cannot live. Also, if the roots are weak, the tree will give little or no fruit.

Father: Okay. Now imagine a person without a heart; Would he live?

Zaid: No, Dad. We need our hearts to stay alive. If the heart is weak, the body will be weak, too. I have a friend in school who has a problem with his heart, so he can't play football with us.

Father: May Allah help him! Iman, my dear, is the heart of Islam. If your iman is strong, your Islam will be strong too.

Zaid: What does the word "iman" mean?

Father: It means faith, or believing in something, even if you don't see it.

Zaid: How can you believe in something that you can't see?

Father: Well, for example, you know that your mom and I love you very much, right?

Zaid: Yes, Dad.

Father: But you do not see our love. Do you?

Zaid: No, but I feel it when you hug me and take care of me!

Creations of God

Father: Do you see God?

Zaid: No, but I know that He is there, in Heaven.

Father: How do you know that?

Zaid: Because I see all the amazing things that Allah ﷻ has created; the birds, the sky, the oceans, the trees, and ME!

Father: So you know that Allah ﷻ is there. And you know that He loves you even more than your parents love you. Do you believe that in your heart?

Zaid: Of course.

Father: Then you have iman. Iman is believing in **God** and every unseen thing He told us about in the Qur'an, even if we cannot see it.

Zaid: Like what?

Father: Like **angels,** *Jannah* (Paradise), ***Jahannam*** (Hell)**, the Day of Judgment,** and *Al-Qadar* (Fate). We do not see these things now, but Allah told us about them. They are called *arkan-ul-iman*, the pillars of faith.

Zaid: Oh, yeah! My Islamic Studies teacher told us that she would teach us those next week, insha Allah.

Allah (is) Al-Mu'min
المـؤمن
THE Faith Giver

WORDS OF WISDOM
Holy Qura'n

سورة البقرة

Surah Al-Baqara 2:285

بِسْمِ ٱللَّهِ ٱلرَّحْمَٰنِ ٱلرَّحِيمِ

﴿ءَامَنَ ٱلرَّسُولُ بِمَآ أُنزِلَ إِلَيْهِ مِن رَّبِّهِ وَٱلْمُؤْمِنُونَ كُلٌّ ءَامَنَ بِٱللَّهِ وَمَلَٰئِكَتِهِ وَكُتُبِهِ وَرُسُلِهِ لَا نُفَرِّقُ بَيْنَ أَحَدٍ مِّن رُّسُلِهِ وَقَالُوا۟ سَمِعْنَا وَأَطَعْنَا غُفْرَانَكَ رَبَّنَا وَإِلَيْكَ ٱلْمَصِيرُ ﴿٢٨٥﴾

TRANSLITERATION

[285] Aman-ar-rasoolu bima onzila ilayhi mir-rabbihi wal-mu'minoona kullun amana billahi wamala'ikatihi waku-tubihi warusulih, la nufarriqu bayna ahadim-mir-rusulih, waqaloo sami'na wa'ata'na, ghufranaka rabbana wa-ilayk-almaseer.

MEANING TRANSLATION

The Messenger has believed in what has been revealed to him from his Lord, and the believers as well. All have believed in Allah and His angels and His Books and His Messengers. "We make no division between any of His Messengers," and they have said: "We have listened, and obeyed. Our Lord, (we seek) Your pardon! And to You is the return." (285)

ACTIVITY time

1. Have your friend tell you about five things that he saw, but you did not. Do you believe that he saw those things?

2. Imagine Islam as a tree, then draw that tree. Show arkanul-islam as its branches, and arkanul-iman as its roots.

3. Imagine Islam as a building, and draw that building. Then show arkanul-islam as its columns, and arkanul-iman as the large blocks of its foundation.

Study Questions

1. What is the heart of Islam?

2. What does iman mean?

3. Can we see iman? Can you feel iman in your heart?

4. What are *arkanul-iman* (pillars of faith)?

الإيـمـان بالله
I Believe In Allah

Questions?

① What is the first pillar of iman?
② Who is Allah?
③ Why do you think that belief in Allah is the first pillar of iman?

Main Idea: Allah is the one and only true God. He created us all. He is the only true God we must worship.

Word
Watch

[Al-Asmaa' -ul-Husna الأسماء الحسنى]

Teacher Hibah started the lesson on arkanul-iman.

Teacher Hibah: Class, we have talked in the past about the five pillars of Islam. Does anyone know what are they called in Arabic?

Class: Arkanul-Islam.

Teacher: Good. Today, we will learn arkanul-iman. This means pillars of faith. Muslims have to believe in these six important things. Can anyone tell us what they are?

Zaid: Yes, my father told me about them.

Teacher Hibah: Good! Tell us, Zaid.

Zaid:

الإيمان بالله	To believe in Allah
الإيمان بملائكته	To believe in Allah's angels
الإيمان بكتبه	To believe in Allah's Books
الإيمان برسله	To believe in Allah's messengers
الإيمان باليوم الآخر	To believe in the Day of Judgment
الإيمان بالقدر، خيره وشره	To believe in fate, the good and the bad.

Teacher Hibah: Great, Zaid! May Allah bless you.

Today we will learned about the first rukn, or pillar, of iman. What is that, class?

Class: Belief in Allah ﷾ .

Teacher Hibah: Great. Jazakumu-Llahu Khairan. (May Allah ﷾ reward you.)

Class: Wa iyyaki. (And you)

Allah ﷻ is the One Who made us all. He also gave the birds wings to fly.

God is the One Who gave the fish in the sea many different colors and shapes.

Allah ﷻ is the One Who created bees and made them produce honey.

God ﷻ is the One Who made the tiny insects and the mighty mountains.

Allah ﷻ is the One Who gave us silk from worms.

Allah ﷻ is the One Who made the flowers blossom with many beautiful colors.

Allah ﷻ is the One Who made delicious fruits grow on trees.

Allah created all of these things for us to use and enjoy. This is why we should thank Allah all the time. We should also treat Allah's creation with respect.

healthy

h a b i t

Always look at Allah's beautiful creations and think about how great Allah is.

Teacher Hibah: Isn't Allah so great, class?

Class: Of course, Teacher!

Teacher: Always remember, Allah ﷻ is ONE. He is the only One God Who created you and me. He is the Most Powerful and no one is like Him. He is the Creator of the Heavens and the Earth, the oceans and the mountains. Allah made humans, jinn, and angels. He also created animals and plants. He made the shining sun, the bright moon, the twinkling stars, and the amazing planets.

NASHEED — Little Star

Twinkle, twinkle, little star
Who has made you what you are?
Shining over land and sea,
Higher than the tallest tree.
Allah has made you and me
Like the star, so perfectly.

Listen to this nasheed on Track 3 of your CD.

Ahmad: WOW, Allah is so great! I love Him so much!

Class: So do we!

Omar: Where is Allah ﷻ ? Can we see Him?

Teacher Hibah: He is in Heaven, and we cannot see him in this life.

Omar: When can we see Him?

Teacher Hibah: Insha Allah, we will see Him when we go to *Jannah* insha Allah.

Zaid: Subhan-Allah, He made this world and *Jannah* for us?

Teacher: Yes, Zaid. You see how great Allah is. Allah is the only one Who can do all. He needs no one to help Him, no partners, no father, no mother and no kids. Every Muslim believes in the only true God - Allah.

Hasan: What does His name Allah mean?

Teacher Hibah: It means "The God to worship."
And by the way class, Allah has 99 names. They are called Al-Asmaa' Al-Husna. This means "the beautiful names."

Bilal: Can you tell us some of those names?

Teacher Hibah: Sure: Al-Quddoos, Al-Kabeer, As-Samad, Al-Azeez, Al-Hameed, and Al-Majeed.

Class: We love Allah.

Teacher Hibah: He loves you too. Class, do you know why Allah created us?

Bilal: Allah created humans to obey and worship Him.

Teacher Hibah: Yes, Bilal. Allah says in Al-Qur'an:

﴿ وَمَا خَلَقْتُ ٱلْجِنَّ وَٱلْإِنسَ إِلَّا لِيَعْبُدُونِ ﴾

"Wama khalaqt-ul-jinna wal-insa illa lya'abudoon."
I did not create the Jinns and the human beings except for the purpose that they should worship Me. (56)
Surah Adh-Dhariyat

So, Allah ﷻ created us on this Earth to worship and obey Him. He wants us to follow His final religion - Al-Islam, His last Book - Al-Qur'an, and His final messenger Muhammad ﷺ .

Think about it!

Why is it wrong to worship more than One God?

Hasan: Teacher Hibah, I wrote a poem about Allah ﷻ. May I read it?
Teacher Hibah: Yes, Hasan!
Hasan:
Allah is one
Allah is one
He has no father
He has no son
He created everything
All the beautiful birds that sing,
The sun, the moon, the Earth, the sea
The oceans, the deserts, You and me!

Class: Allahu Akbar!
Teacher Hibah: Great Hassan, may Allah bless you! Class, we have a great new student this year, alhamdulillah.

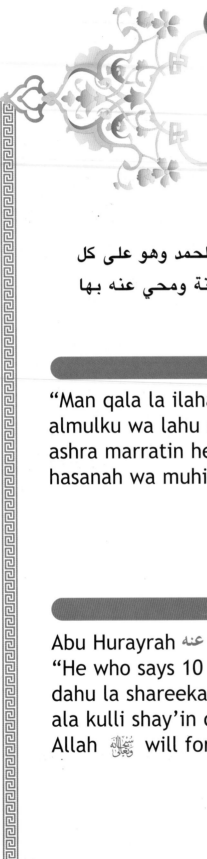

WORDS OF WISDOM
Hadeeth Shareef

حديث شريف

Narrated By Bukhari & Muslim

عن أبي هريرة رضي الله عنه: قال رسول الله ﷺ :
"من قال لا إله إلا الله وحده لا شريك له له الملك وله الحمد وهو على كل
شئ قدير عشر مرات حين يصبح كتب له بها مائة حسنة ومحي عنه بها
مائة سيئة."

TRANSLITERATION

"Man qala la ilaha ill-Allah wahdahu la shareeka lahu lahu
almulku wa lahu alhamdu wa howa ala kulli shay'in qadeer,
ashra marratin heena yusbih, kutiba lahu biha mi'atu
hasanah wa muhiya 'anhu biha mi'atu sayi'ah."

MEANING TRANSLATION

Abu Hurayrah رضي الله عنه reported that the Prophet ﷺ said:
"He who says 10 times in the morning "la Ilaha Ill-Allah wahdahu la shareeka lah, lahul-maulku wa laul hamdu wahuwa
ala kulli shay'in qadeer," will be given 100 rewards, and
Allah ﷻ will forgive 100 of his sins.

ACTIVITY time

Make a colorful poster of some of the names of Allah and some of His beautiful creations.

healthy habit

Say every day 10 times:

لا إله إلا الله وحده لا شريك له، له الملك وله الحمد وهو على كل شيئ قدير

La ilaha illallah wahdahu la sharee-ka lah, lahul-mulku wa lahul-hamdu, wa huwa ala kulli shay'in Qadeer.

This means: There is no God but Allah. His is all the power, and His is all the praise, and He is capable of doing everything.

It takes only one minute to do this, but you will get a wonderful reward!

Study  Questions

1   What is the first rukn of *arkanul-iman*?

2   Who is Allah ﷻ, and where is He?

3   What do we call the names of Allah in Arabic? Name some.

4   Can we ever see Allah? When and where?

5   Why did Allah create us?

الإيمان بالملائكة
Allah's Angels

Questions?

1. What are angels?
2. What is the Arabic word for angels?
3. Do Muslims have to believe in angels?
4. What are angels made of?
5. Are there angels around us?

Main Idea: Belief in Allah's angels is one of the six pillars of *iman*. As Muslims, we believe that there are many angels all around us.

Word
Watch

Malak	مَلَك
Mala'ikah	ملائكة
Noor	نـور
Al-Bayt-ul-Ma'mour	البيت المعمور

Do you know what angels are?

Allah made so many creatures. He created humans, *jinn*, and angels. Angels are one of God's amazing creations. Allah tells us in the Holy Qur'an that angels are made of light (*Noor*).

Sometimes we see pictures of angels in books or magazines. But these pictures are not correct. No one really knows how Allah's real angels look. The pictures we see are just drawings from someone's imagination.

Think about it!

Why do people like to imagine how angels look?

The Qur'an tells us that angels can take different shapes and forms. And we know that they have wings. Sometimes they have two, sometimes four, sometimes even more, as Allah said in the Qur'an. The Angel Jibreel (Gabriel) has 600 wings, as Prophet Muhammad ﷺ once said!

Allah has given angels many jobs to do, and they do them without complaining or arguing. Angels do not need to eat or sleep. They do not get tired. They worship Allah ﷻ all the time. They have their own prayers and *tasbeeh* (translation: "remembrances of Allah"). The angels do the same job all day, everyday, until the end of time.

healthy
habit

When you are asked to do a good thing, do it well and finish your job without arguing or complaining. This is what the angels do.

What is the Arabic word for angels?

Mala'ikah is the Arabic word for angels. One angel is called malak.

I HAVE GUARDIAN ANGELS

Allah ﷻ loves us so much that He gave each one of us two angels; one in front of us, and one behind us. They protect us from harm and take care of us. They are called "the Guardian Angels." We love our guardian angels.

MY GOOD AND BAD DEEDS

Allah also gave each of us two other angels at our sides. They record our deeds, both good and bad. They are called "the Honorable Writing Angels." They record everything we say and do. The angel on the right writes down the good deeds. And the angel on the left writes down the bad deeds.

Who is the leader of the angels?

The leader of the angels is Jibreel عليه السلام. Angel Jibreel has 600 wings. He is the angel who delivered the message from Allah to all the prophets.

The following are the names of some angels and their duties:

Jibreel عليه السلام ....He brought God's Books to the Messengers
Mika'eel عليه السلام ....He takes care of rain, upon orders from Allah
Israfeel عليه السلام ....With the permission of Allah سبحانه وتعالى , he will blow the trumpet on the Day of Judgment
Ridwan عليه السلام ....He is the guardian of Paradise (*Jannah*)
Malik عليه السلام .... He is the guardian of Hellfire
Angel of Death عليه السلام ....He takes humans' souls at the time of death. Some scholars call him Izra'eel!!

My Two Angels

I have two angels that follow me
wherever I may go.
One of them is quick to write,
the other one is slow
The one who is quick to write
is when I'm being good.
The other doesn't like to write,
even when he should!
The one who doesn't like to write
is when I'm being bad.
He wants to hear me say "I'm sorry"
to my mom and dad.
And when I say "I'm sorry, Allah!
I won't do that again,"
he rubs away the bad deed
marked against my name.
The one who is quick to write
writes the good I try to do.
Even, when it doesn't work out just right,
he writes that one down too.
So when I get to Paradise,
waiting there for me
will be lots of lovely presents -
oh, how happy I will be!

AL-BAYT UL-MA'MOUR

Al-Bayt ul-Ma'mour is the house of worship for the angels. It is like Al-Ka'ba of the Heavens. Seventy thousand new angels make hajj to *Al-Bayt ul-Ma'mour* every day.

Do we know how many angels there are?

There are so many angels created by Allah ﷻ . No one knows exactly how many there are, except Allah ﷻ .

What is your duty toward the angels?

My duty is to believe in them. I must also love and respect them. Also, I should not keep them busy writing my bad deeds; they don't like that. They only like to write good deeds.

Study  Questions

1 What are angels made of?

2 Why do Muslims have to believe in angels?

3 What are writing angels? How many do we have?

4 What are guardian angels?

5 Who is Jibreel?

6 Name 3 angels and explain their jobs.

الإيـمان بالكتب
The Books of Allah

Questions?

① What would you do to teach others something important?
② What are the Books of Allah ﷻ? Why did Allah send these Books?
③ What was the Book sent to Prophet Muhammad?
④ Is Al-Qur'an only for reading?

Main Idea: Allah sent down many Books to teach and remind people to worship Him and do good deeds. Muslims believe in and respect all of Allah's Books, but the Qur'an is the final, true, and unchanged Word of God.

Word Watch

Al-Qur'an	القرآن
Ayah (Verse)	آيـة
Ayaat (Verses)	آيـات
Surah (Chapter)	سـورة
Suwar (Chapters)	سـور
Tawrah (Torah)	تـوراه
Injeel (Bible)	إنـجيل
Zaboor (Psalms)	زبـور

Have you ever been to a new school and gotten lost?

Did you have to ask someone to help you find your classroom or the library?

Was it hard to figure out which way to go?

Why did Allah send His Books to people?

Have you ever been lost? Even grown-ups get lost sometimes when they go places. They use maps or ask for directions when they need help.

Allah ﷻ does not want people to get lost in this life. He has given us Books that teach us how to have a good and peaceful life on Earth.

These Books teach us how to worship Allah ﷻ and do the right things in our daily life. If we do what Allah ﷻ teaches us, we will be happy in this life and go to *Jannah* after we die.

How did people get the Books of Allah?

Allah ﷻ chose some prophets to teach people His Books. Allah sent Angel Jibreel عليه السلام to teach the prophets the Books. The prophets loved God's words and learned the Books by heart. Then the prophets taught their people the Books of Allah.

We do not know what happened to some of the Books, like the *Suhuf*, or scrolls of Ibraheem. These Books were apparently lost. Others were changed by people after their prophets passed away. The only Book that is still complete and unchanged is the Holy Qur'an.

Allah taught Al-Qur'an to Prophet Muhammad ﷺ. Muhammad ﷺ was the last Prophet of Allah. Al-Qur'an was also the last Book of Allah. Muslims wrote down the whole Book before Prophet Muhammad ﷺ passed away. They kept the first copy in a very safe place.

Muslims throughout the years have memorized the whole Qur'an by heart. They have also made many copies of it and kept them in masajid, homes, and schools. Now, people print Al-Qur'an into Books like the ones you have at home. We even have Al-Qur'an available on computers now.

In Al-Qur'an, Allah ﷻ tells us about other Books, which He revealed to His prophets a long time ago.

Name of the Book			This Book was given to Prophet		
As-Suhuf	الصحف	(Books)	Ibraheem	إبراهيم	(Abraham)
At-Tawrah	التوراه	(Torah)	Musa	موسى	(Moses)
Az-Zaboor	الزبور	(Psalms)	Dawood	داود	(David)
Al-Injeel	الإنجيل	(Bible)	Isa	عيسى	(Jesus)
Al-Qur'an	القرآن		Muhammad	محمد	

عليهم السلام

Peace be upon them all.

healthy

h a b i t

Always show respect to Al-Qur'an by doing the following:
— Read it, learn it, memorize it, practice it, and always keep it in a safe, clean, and high place.

What is Al-Qur'an?

Al-Qur'an contains the Words of Allah, and It is His final Book. It is the greatest Book ever. Muslims should read it, learn it by heart, respect it, and follow its teachings.

Al-Qur'an was revealed in the Arabic language. Allah has promised to protect the Qur'an from any change or loss.

﴾ إِنَّا نَحْنُ نَزَّلْنَا الذِّكْرَ وَإِنَّا لَهُ لَحَافِظُونَ ﴿

"Inna nahnu nazzalna-thikra wa inna lahu lahafidhoon"

We, Ourselves, have sent down the Dhikr (the Qur'an), and We are there to protect it. (9 Surah Al-Hijr

No one can change Al-Qur'an. No one can write anything like it, not even one surah or chapter. Al-Qur'an has 114 suwar, or chapters, and more than 6000 ayat, or verses.

Zaid: Why can't anyone write a Book like Al-Qur'an?
Father: Can anyone do what Allah ﷻ does?
Zaid: No, no one can.
Father: Allah wrote Al-Qur'an, so no one else can write anything like it, either!

REMEMBER

Belief in all of Allah's revealed Books is an important part of *iman*. It is one of the six pillars of *iman*, and *iman* is the heart of Islam.

سورة الأعلى

Surah Al-Ala 87: 1-19

بِسْمِ اللَّهِ الرَّحْمَٰنِ الرَّحِيمِ

سَبِّحِ اسْمَ رَبِّكَ الْأَعْلَى ۝ الَّذِي خَلَقَ فَسَوَّىٰ ۝ وَالَّذِي قَدَّرَ فَهَدَىٰ ۝ وَالَّذِي أَخْرَجَ الْمَرْعَىٰ ۝ فَجَعَلَهُ غُثَاءً أَحْوَىٰ ۝ سَنُقْرِئُكَ فَلَا تَنسَىٰ ۝ إِلَّا مَا شَاءَ اللَّهُ إِنَّهُ يَعْلَمُ الْجَهْرَ وَمَا يَخْفَىٰ ۝ وَنُيَسِّرُكَ لِلْيُسْرَىٰ ۝ فَذَكِّرْ إِن نَّفَعَتِ الذِّكْرَىٰ ۝ سَيَذَّكَّرُ مَن يَخْشَىٰ ۝ وَيَتَجَنَّبُهَا الْأَشْقَى ۝ الَّذِي يَصْلَى النَّارَ الْكُبْرَىٰ ۝ ثُمَّ لَا يَمُوتُ فِيهَا وَلَا يَحْيَىٰ ۝ قَدْ أَفْلَحَ مَن تَزَكَّىٰ ۝ وَذَكَرَ اسْمَ رَبِّهِ فَصَلَّىٰ ۝ بَلْ تُؤْثِرُونَ الْحَيَاةَ الدُّنْيَا ۝ وَالْآخِرَةُ خَيْرٌ وَأَبْقَىٰ ۝ إِنَّ هَٰذَا لَفِي الصُّحُفِ الْأُولَىٰ ۝ صُحُفِ إِبْرَاهِيمَ وَمُوسَىٰ ۝

TRANSLITERATION

1. Sabbih-isma rabbik al-'a'la
2. Allathee khalaqa fasaww
3. Wallathee qaddara fahada
4. Waallathee akhraj-almar'a
5. Faja'alahu ghutha'an ahwa
6. Sanuqri'oka fala tansa
7. Illa masha Allahu innahu ya'lam-ul-jahra wama yakhfa
8. Wanuyassiruka lilyusra
9. Fathakkir in nafa'at-ith-thikra
10. Sayththakkaru mey-yakhsha
11. Wayatajannabuhal-ashqa
12. Allathee yasla-nnar-alkubra

13. Thumma layamootu feeha wala yahya
14. Qad aflaha man tazakka
15. Wathakar-asma rabbihi fasalla
16. Bal tu'thiroon-alhayat-addunya
17. Wal-'akhiratu khayrun wa'abqa
18. Inna hatha lafi-ssuhuf-il-'oola
19. Suhufi ibraheema wamoosa

Pronounce the purity of the name of your most exalted Lord, (1) Who created (everything), then made (it) well, (2)And who determined a measure (for everything), then guided (it), (3) And who brought forth pasturage, (4) Then turned it into a blackening stubble. (5) We will make you recite, then you will not forget (6) Except that which Allah wills. Indeed He knows what is manifest and what is hidden. (7) And We will facilitate for you (to reach) the easiest way. (8) So, extend advice (to people) if advice is useful. (9) The one who fears (Allah) will observe the advice, (10) And it will be avoided by the most wretched one (11) Who will enter the Biggest Fire, (12) Then he will neither die therein, nor live (a desirable life). (13) Success is surely achieved by him who purifies himself, (14) And pronounces the name of his Lord, then offers prayer. (15) But you prefer the worldly life, (16) While the Hereafter is much better and much more durable. (17) Indeed this is (written) in the earlier divine scripts, (18) The scripts of Ibrahim and Musa. (19)

ACTIVITY time

Open Al-Qur'an and count the suwar.
Also, see which is the longest surah and
which is the shortest.

Study Questions

1. Why did Allah send His Books to people?

2. Name the Books that were sent to the prophets before Prophet Muhammad ﷺ .

3. What is the name of the Book that was sent to Prophet Muhammad ﷺ ? How is it special?

4. Why should we read Al-Qur'an?

5. How many suwar (chapters) are in Al-Qur'an? And how many ayat (verses) are in it?

6. Can anyone write a Book like Al-Qur'an? Why not?

الإيمان بالأنبياء والرسل
Prophets and Messengers

Questions?

1 Who are the prophets?
2 Why did Allah send prophets?
3 What are the names of some prophets of Allah?

Main Idea: Allah ﷻ chose prophets and messengers to teach people how to worship and do good deeds in this life. Muslims must believe in all the prophets. We must also follow the guidance of Prophet Muhammad ﷺ, the last of Allah's messengers.

Word Watch

Nabiyy (Prophet)	نبي
Anbiya'	أنبياء
Rasool (Messenger)	رسول
Rusul	رُسُل
Hasanat	حسنات
Tawheed	توحيد

Zaid, Bilal and Hasan went to the masjid. After they prayed Asr, they sat for their weekly lesson. Their teacher Isa greeted them.

Teacher Isa: Assalamu alaykum, young brothers.
Group: Wa alaykum assalam wa rahmatullahi wabarakatuh.
Teacher Isa: Welcome to our weekly lesson in the masjid. I am proud of you all because you like to pray in the masjid and attend this lesson.
Zaid: We all love the masjid; it is the House of Allah.
Hasan: We come here to gain *hasanat* (good deeds). I want to collect a lot of hasanat so I can go to *Jannah*.
Bilal: I heard that every time you go to the masjid, Allah builds you a palace in *Jannah*.
Teacher Isa: That's true, Bilal. Now let's start. Boys, what is my name?
Group: Your name is Teacher Isa.
Teacher Isa: Do you know why I have that name?
Bilal: Because your parents gave it to you.

Teacher: That's right, but my parents gave me this name because it was the name of Prophet Isa عليه السلام. He was one of the greatest prophets of Allah. Today we will learn about these prophets. Do you know what the Arabic word for prophet is?

Hasan: Nabiy.

Zaid: It can also be *rasool*.

Teacher Isa:Yes, a prophet is called Nabiy and a messenger is called rasool. Anbiyaa' is the plural of nabiy, and rusul is the plural of rasool. You should know that a nabiy is a prophet who is only asked to deliver the message of Islam to his family and people in his area. He is ordered to teach his family and his people in the surroundings to practice Islam and be good examples to others. An example of a prophet is Prophet Adam. He and his family were alone on Earth.

A *rasool*, or messenger, however, is ordered to teach many more people. He is required to teach his whole nation and region the message of Allah. Prophets Musa and 'Isa عليه السلام, for example, were sent to the Children of Israel. One rasool was sent with the Last Book to all the people around the world from his time to the end of time. Who was that?

Bilal: That was Prophet Muhammad ﷺ .

Teacher Isa: Great, Bilal. Prophet Muhammad was sent to all mankind. That is why there was no Prophet or messenger sent after Prophet Muhammad ﷺ . A messenger can also be called a prophet, but a prophet cannot be called a messenger. So, every rasool is a nabiy, but not every nabiy is a *rasool*.

Some *rusul* have received Books from Allah, like the Torah, Injeel, and the Qur'an. Most rusul did not receive Books. They only received new verbal instructions, or they were ordered to follow Books sent to previous messengers.

The job of rusul was to deliver the Message of Allah ﷻ, to teach people how to behave the best way on Earth, and to be ready for the hereafter.

Every prophet spoke the language of his people. They all came with the same message of Tawheed. They wanted to remind people that they should only worship the one true God, Allah. At the end, Allah chose Muhammad ﷺ to be the final prophet and messenger. He was sent to all of mankind for the rest of time.

Think about it!

Why do you think people kept forgetting the message that was brought to them by the prophets?

Why do you think Allah kept reminding people about the message?

Zaid: How many prophets did Allah send?

Teacher Isa: Allah sent so many prophets to teach mankind. There are thousands of prophets of Allah ﷻ.
Allah mentioned the names of 25 prophets in the Holy Qur'an.
Can you name some of the great prophets?

Hasan: Adam, Nouh, Ibraheem..

Zaid: Also, Ismail, Ishaq, Dawood, Solayman, Ya'qoob, Yousuf, Hood, Salih...

Teacher Isa: Can anyone name some prophets who received Books from Allah?

Bilal: Ibraheem, Musa, Isa, Muhammad.

Teacher Isa: All right. There are other prophets like Zakariyya, Yahya, Idrees, Loot, Ayyoob, Younus, Haroon, Ilyas, Shu'ayb, Thul-Kifl, Alyasa', and the Final Prophet, of course, Muhammad, peace and blessings of Allah be upon all of them. Let's look at this chart; it lists all of the Prophets of Allah who are named in the Qur'an.

PROPHETS OF ALLAH

1 Adam	2 Idrees	3 Nouh
4 Houd	5 Salih	6 Ibraheem
7 Lout	8 Isma'eel	9 Is-haq
10 Ya'qoob	11 Yousuf	12 Ayyoob
13 Thul-kifl	14 Shu'ayb	15 Moosa
16 Haroun	17 Dawoud	18 Sulayman
19 Ilyas	20 Alyasa'	21 Younus
22 Zakariyya	23 Yahya	24 Isa

25 Muhammad

Peace Be Upon All of Them

Allah ﷻ sent His final and last message of Islam to all mankind through Prophet Muhammad ﷺ .

As a Muslim,

I should love and respect all of the Prophets of Allah. May Allah reward them for all that they have done.

healthy

h a b i t

Every time you say or hear the name of a prophet, say:

عليه السَّلام

"Peace be upon him

Alayhi as-Salam

ACTIVITY time

Choose a prophet and summarize his story. Who was he sent to? Why was he sent?

Study Questions

1 Why did Allah send prophets?

2 How many prophets' names are mentioned in the Qur'an?

3 Name ten prophets. Name three messengers.

4 What is the Arabic word for prophet? What is the Arabic word for messenger?

الإيمان باليوم الآخر
Yawm-ul-Qiyamah - The Day of Judgment

Questions?

1. What should we do if we make a mistake?
2. What is Yawmul Qiyamah?
3. What are some signs of that day?

Main Idea: All of our deeds are recorded. On the Day of Judgment we will answer for all of our deeds, both good and bad.

Word Watch

Yawm ul-Qiyamah	يوم القيامة
Israfeel	إسرافيل
Day of Judgement	يوم الحساب
Book of Deeds	كتاب الأعمال

Bilal came to his mom crying. She could not understand what had happened to him. He was talking and crying at the same time.

Mother: What happened, Bilal. What's wrong?

Bilal could not speak clearly because he was still crying.
Mother: Calm down, Bilal, and then talk!

Bilal: Somebody stole my ball.

Mother: Who was it?

Bilal: I don't know. Some older kids came to me outside and took my ball. They pushed me hard and made me fall.

Mother: Are you sure you don't know who they are?

Bilal: No, Mom. But I really want to get my ball back.

Mother: I'll ask your dad to find them.

Bilal: What if he can't find them?

Mother: Then, we will meet them on *Yawm ul-Qiyamah*.

Bilal: What is that?

Mother: We were all created by Allah ﷻ, and to Him we shall return after we die. The day when everybody is gathered to Allah ﷻ is called *Yawmul-Qiyamah*, the Day of Judgment.

Bilal: When is that?

Mother: We don't know. One day in the future. On that Last Day, Allah will order Angel Israfeel to blow the trumpet to start the Day of Judgment.
On that day, mountains will float like cotton and dust, the sun and the moon will disappear, and the whole universe will be destroyed. Then everyone will be raised from their graves and stand humbly before Allah ﷻ.

Bilal: Will I get my ball back them?

Mother: The ball will show up in the Book of Deeds of the boys who stole it.

Bilal: What Book?

Mother: On the Day of Judgment, everybody will receive his or her Book of Deeds. Those who obeyed Allah ﷻ and did many good deeds will receive their Book with their right hand. And those who did not obey Allah and did many bad deeds will receive their Books in their left hand.

Bilal: Will the bad boys see my ball in their bad deeds?

Mother: Yes, and they will be very sorry. They may beg you to forgive them.

Bilal: I will never forgive them.
Mother: Wait. You may also see something else in your Book of Good deeds.

Bilal: What is that?
Mother: Many *hasanat*; if you are patient and trust that Allah ﷻ will give something better than your ball somehow. Also, if you forgive these boys on the Day of Judgment, Allah ﷻ will give you things in *Jannah* that will be much better than your ball.

Bilal: Better than my ball?

Mother: Much, much better.
Bilal: I trust Allah, but it will be hard to forgive the boys who took my ball.

WORDS OF WISDOM

Holy Qura'n

سورة القارعة

Surah Al-Qaria 101: 1-11

ٱلْقَارِعَةُ ﴿١﴾ مَا ٱلْقَارِعَةُ ﴿٢﴾ وَمَآ أَدْرَىٰكَ مَا ٱلْقَارِعَةُ ﴿٣﴾ يَوْمَ يَكُونُ ٱلنَّاسُ كَٱلْفَرَاشِ ٱلْمَبْثُوثِ ﴿٤﴾ وَتَكُونُ ٱلْجِبَالُ كَٱلْعِهْنِ ٱلْمَنفُوشِ ﴿٥﴾ فَأَمَّا مَن ثَقُلَتْ مَوَٰزِينُهُۥ ﴿٦﴾ فَهُوَ فِي عِيشَةٍ رَّاضِيَةٍ ﴿٧﴾ وَأَمَّا مَنْ خَفَّتْ مَوَٰزِينُهُۥ ﴿٨﴾ فَأُمُّهُۥ هَاوِيَةٌ ﴿٩﴾ وَمَآ أَدْرَىٰكَ مَا هِيَهْ ﴿١٠﴾ نَارٌ حَامِيَةٌ ﴿١١﴾

TRANSLITERATION

[1] Alqari'ah
[2] Malqari'ah
[3] Wama 'adr aka malqari'ah
[4] Yawma yakoon-un-nasu kalfarash-il-mabthooth
[5] Watakoon-ul-jibalu kal'ihn-il-manfoosh
[6] Fa'amma man thaqulat mawazeenuh
[7] Fahuwa fee 'eeshatin radiyah
[8] Wa'amma man khaffat mawazeenuh
[9] Fa'ommuhu hawiyah
[10] Wama adraka ma hiyah
[11] Narun hamiyatun

MEANING TRANSLATION

The Striking Event! (1) What is the Striking Event? (2) And what may let you know what the Striking Event is? (3) It will happen) on a day when people will be like scattered moths, (4) And the mountains will be like carded wool. (5)Then, as for him whose scales (of good deeds) are heavy, (6) He will be in a happy life. (7) But he whose scales are light, (8) His abode will be Abyss. (9) And what may let you know what that (Abyss) is? (10) A blazing Fire! (11)

The door bell rang, and Bilal ran to open it. His mother followed him.

Mrs. Ameen: Assalamu alaykum. I am Mrs. Ameen. We live on the next street. My son did something really inappropriate.

Mother: Wa alaykum assalam, Sister. Please come in. Please sit down.

Mrs. Ameen: *Jazakumu-llahu khairan*, Sister. I am so sorry for what my son Layth did. I asked him about the new ball he just brought home, and I found out that he stole it from your son. I was so ashamed and upset.

Bilal: He also pushed me and made me fall. My leg still hurts.

Mrs. Ameen: I am so sorry, Dear. We came to give you your ball back. Layth also hopes that you will forgive him.

Layth: I am sorry, Bilal. Please forgive me. I know that I did something bad. Here is your ball.

Bilal looked at his mom. She smiled and nodded.

Bilal: All right. I forgive you. You don't have to steal my ball. You can play with me anytime. I want Allah to give me hasanat so I can go to *Jannah* on the Day of Judgment. Also, I don't want you to have bad deeds in your Book of Deeds.

Layth: Thank you.

Mother: Bilal, why don't you play with Layth outside. I will fix Mrs. Ameen something to drink.

healthy
habit

When you make a mistake towards others:
1. Admit it.
2. Make istighfar, and seek forgiveness from Allah.
3. Seek the forgiveness of the person whom you hurt.
4. Try not to make the same mistake again. Remember that we all make mistakes, and Allah is kind and forgiving. We just have to ask for His forgiveness. Let's keep our Book of Deeds free from bad deeds.

سورة الزلزلة

Al-Zalzala 99: 1-8

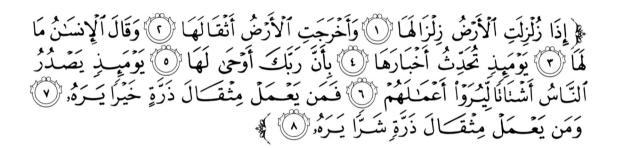

TRANSLITERATION

[1] Itha zulzilat-il-ardu zilzalaha

[2] Waakhrajat-il-'ardu athqalaha

[3] Waqal al-insanu malaha

[4] Yawma-'ithin tuhaddithu akhbaraha

[5] Bi-anna rabbaka awhalaha

[6] Yawma-ithiy yasdur-un-nasu 'ashtatal liyuraw a'malahum

[7] Famay ya'mal mithqala tharratin khayray yarah

[8] Waman ya'mal mithqala tharratin sharray yarah

MEANING TRANSLATION

When the earth will be trembled with its quake, (1) And the earth will bring forth its burdens, (2) And man will say, "What has happened to it?" (3) That day it will describe all its happenings, (4) Because its Lord will have so commanded it. (5) That day the people will come back (from the place of reckoning) in different groups, so that they may be shown (the fruits of) their deeds. (6) So, whoever does any good act (even) to the weight of a particle will see it. (7) And whoever does evil (even) to the weight of a particle will see it. (8)

الـخـافـض

الرافع

The one who can bring high things down, and make powerful people weak.

The one who can bring low things up, and make weak people powerful.

Thinking Critically

Why is it important to believe in the Day of Judgment?

1. Collect pictures of the destruction that earthquakes caused to land and buildings. Discuss the quake of *Yawm ul-Qiyamah* with your classmates.

2. Watch a documentary about earthquakes. Think about how much worse the quake of *Yawm ul-Qiyamah* will be.

Study Questions

1. What is *Yawm ul-Qiyamah*?

2. Why is it important to believe in *Yawm ul-Qiyamah*?

3. What should a Muslim do when he or she makes a mistake?

4. What is the name of the angel who blows the trumpet on the Day of Judgment?

الإيـمان بـالقدر
Al-Qadar: Fate

Questions?

① What should a Muslim do if something bad happens?
② Who controls the whole universe?
③ What is Al-Qadar?

Main Idea: Muslims know that nothing can happen without Allah's permission, and Allah knows everything that will happen in every time and place.

Word Watch

Al-Qadar	القَدَر
Istighfar	إستِغفار
Al-Ajal	الأجَل
Ar-Rizq	الرِّزق
As-Sihhah	الصِّحَّة

What does Al-Qadar mean?

Al-Qadar means fate.
This means that Allah ﷻ controls the fate of people and the whole universe. Everything happens with His knowledge and permission. He knows everything that happened in the past, He knows everything that is happening now, and He knows everything that will happen in the future. Nothing happens in this world without His permission.

Allah is the only one who decides the following:

- **Al-Ajal** or life span: How long we live and when we will die.

- **As-Sihhah** or health: When we get sick and when we recover.

- **Ar-Rizq** or wealth: how much money we will earn.

- **Life Quality:** Happiness, or living with a struggle.

People can choose to do what is right in this life, or choose to do what is wrong. Allah gave people the choice to do good or bad deeds. People choose to pray or not pray, to lie or tell the truth, to work hard for Islam or to be lazy and do little. However, when we do good deeds we will be rewarded, and when you do bad deeds, we may be punished.

We should believe that everything that happens to us comes from Allah ﷻ . When something good happens to us and we like it, we should say "Alhamdulillah" الحمد لله . If something bad happens to us, we should accept it, be patient, ask Allah ﷻ for help, and also say "Alhamdulillah" الحمد لله. Sometimes bad things happen to us because we did bad things, and Allah is unhappy with us. Sometimes Allah wants to make us stronger and smarter. Difficult times make people work harder and learn better life skills. They learn what is good for them and what is bad, what is safe and what is unsafe.

It could have been worse

Leena was riding her bicycle when she fell and broke her leg very badly. Her bicycle was broken too. Leena had to stay in bed for a short while. She felt very bad. She wished she could get up and play with her friends.

Leena: "Why did my leg have to break?"
Father: We should not complain and ask why something has happened to us, because Allah knows best.

Leena's father went to the library and brought a videotape of handicapped children who used wheelchairs and could not walk. The whole family sat down and watched the video together. The video showed the children using their wheelchairs. They were happy and were doing all kinds of things. They were even playing basketball.

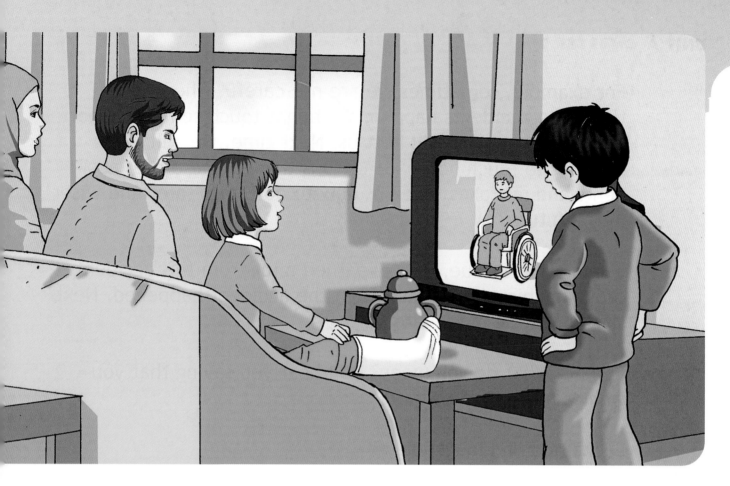

When the movie was over, Leena's dad said to her:

Father: My dear Leena, a few more weeks and you will be up on your feet and running again. Many children do not have this chance. Your injury could have been worse.

Nodding her head, Leena said some istighfar. She asked Allah to forgive her, then said "Alhamdulillah my other leg is good." Leena believed in "Al-Qadar."

Leena: Dad, I just want to understand why bad things happen to us sometimes.
Father: Good question, Leena. Sometimes Allah wants us to become stronger. When we go through tough times, we work harder and act smarter, so we become stronger and smarter in the future. In addition, sometimes Allah is testing us to see if we are patient and respectful during difficult times. Allah tests those He loves to make them stronger and prove their faith in Him.

For example, sometimes we are not careful when we do things, so accidents happen. We might touch something hot on the stove and it will hurt us. Next time, we will make sure not to touch hot or dangerous things. Therefore, accidents and mistakes teach us how to do things safer and wiser in the future.

Leena: That is true, Dad. I learned a lot from this accident. I drove my bicycle too fast when the accident happened. Next time, I will be more careful.

Father: What do you mean? Do I hear you saying that you want a new bicycle?

Leena and dad laughed.

Only Allah

Once Abdullah Ibn Ibbas, the cousin of Prophet Muhammad, rode a camel behind the Prophet. Abdullah was very happy. He used to love the Prophet very much. The Prophet asked Abdullah, "Would you like me to teach you some good words, Abdullah?"
"Yes, "Abdullah happily answered." So the Prophet said, "Obey Allah, and He will protect you. Obey Allah always so He will be there for you whenever you need Him. If you need something, ask Allah. If you seek help, seek the help of Allah. And know that even if all people gather to help you with anything, they will not be able to help you unless Allah has written it for you. And know that if they all gather to harm you, they will not be able to harm you unless Allah has written that for you."

The Prophet continued:

"Obey Allah in easy times. He will help you when you have difficult times. Nothing will happen to you if Allah doesn't want it to happen. And if Allah wants something to happen to you, it will not pass you by.

Know that Allah gives victory with perseverance, relief comes with hardship, and ease comes with difficulty."

Abdullah was happy to learn this great wisdom. He made sure throughout his whole life to do exactly what Prophet Muhammad advised him to do.

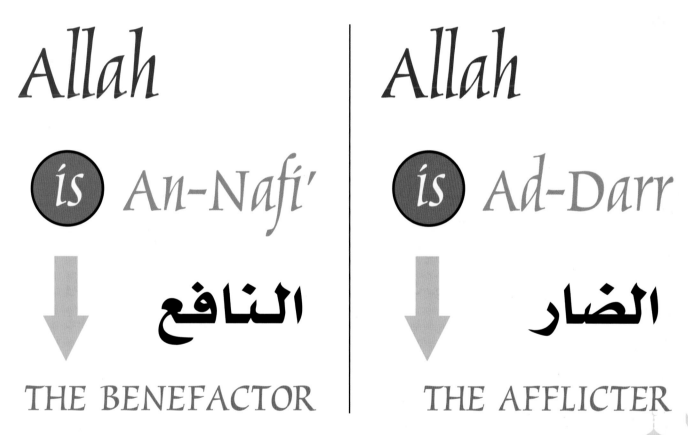

Allah is An-Nafi'	Allah is Ad-Darr
النافع	الضار
THE BENEFACTOR	THE AFFLICTER

He is the one who can really benefit us or inflict harm upon us. Allah ﷻ says to Muhammad ﷺ: "I have no power to bring a benefit or a harm to myself, except that which Allah wills..." (188)
Al-Araf 7:188

WORDS OF WISDOM
Holy Qura'n

سورة الفجر

Al-Fajr 89: 1-30

بِسْمِ اللَّهِ الرَّحْمَٰنِ الرَّحِيمِ

وَالْفَجْرِ ﴿١﴾ وَلَيَالٍ عَشْرٍ ﴿٢﴾ وَالشَّفْعِ وَالْوَتْرِ ﴿٣﴾ وَاللَّيْلِ إِذَا يَسْرِ ﴿٤﴾ هَلْ فِي ذَٰلِكَ قَسَمٌ لِّذِي حِجْرٍ ﴿٥﴾ أَلَمْ تَرَ كَيْفَ فَعَلَ رَبُّكَ بِعَادٍ ﴿٦﴾ إِرَمَ ذَاتِ الْعِمَادِ ﴿٧﴾ الَّتِي لَمْ يُخْلَقْ مِثْلُهَا فِي الْبِلَادِ ﴿٨﴾ وَثَمُودَ الَّذِينَ جَابُوا الصَّخْرَ بِالْوَادِ ﴿٩﴾ وَفِرْعَوْنَ ذِي الْأَوْتَادِ ﴿١٠﴾ الَّذِينَ طَغَوْا فِي الْبِلَادِ ﴿١١﴾ فَأَكْثَرُوا فِيهَا الْفَسَادَ ﴿١٢﴾ فَصَبَّ عَلَيْهِمْ رَبُّكَ سَوْطَ عَذَابٍ ﴿١٣﴾ إِنَّ رَبَّكَ لَبِالْمِرْصَادِ ﴿١٤﴾ فَأَمَّا الْإِنسَانُ إِذَا مَا ابْتَلَاهُ رَبُّهُ فَأَكْرَمَهُ وَنَعَّمَهُ فَيَقُولُ رَبِّي أَكْرَمَنِ ﴿١٥﴾ وَأَمَّا إِذَا مَا ابْتَلَاهُ فَقَدَرَ عَلَيْهِ رِزْقَهُ فَيَقُولُ رَبِّي أَهَانَنِ ﴿١٦﴾ كَلَّا ۖ بَل لَّا تُكْرِمُونَ الْيَتِيمَ ﴿١٧﴾ وَلَا تَحَاضُّونَ عَلَىٰ طَعَامِ الْمِسْكِينِ ﴿١٨﴾ وَتَأْكُلُونَ التُّرَاثَ أَكْلًا لَّمًّا ﴿١٩﴾ وَتُحِبُّونَ الْمَالَ حُبًّا جَمًّا ﴿٢٠﴾ كَلَّا إِذَا دُكَّتِ الْأَرْضُ دَكًّا دَكًّا ﴿٢١﴾ وَجَاءَ رَبُّكَ وَالْمَلَكُ صَفًّا صَفًّا ﴿٢٢﴾ وَجِيءَ يَوْمَئِذٍ بِجَهَنَّمَ ۚ يَوْمَئِذٍ يَتَذَكَّرُ الْإِنسَانُ وَأَنَّىٰ لَهُ الذِّكْرَىٰ ﴿٢٣﴾ يَقُولُ يَا لَيْتَنِي قَدَّمْتُ لِحَيَاتِي ﴿٢٤﴾ فَيَوْمَئِذٍ لَّا يُعَذِّبُ عَذَابَهُ أَحَدٌ ﴿٢٥﴾ وَلَا يُوثِقُ وَثَاقَهُ أَحَدٌ ﴿٢٦﴾ يَا أَيَّتُهَا النَّفْسُ الْمُطْمَئِنَّةُ ﴿٢٧﴾ ارْجِعِي إِلَىٰ رَبِّكِ رَاضِيَةً مَّرْضِيَّةً ﴿٢٨﴾ فَادْخُلِي فِي عِبَادِي ﴿٢٩﴾ وَادْخُلِي جَنَّتِي ﴿٣٠﴾

89:1 Walfajr
89:2 Walayalin ashr
89:3 Washshaf'i walwatr
89:4 Wallayli itha yasr
89:5 Hal fee thalika qasamun lithee hijr
89:6 Alam tara kayfa fa'ala rabbuka bi'ad
89:7 Irama thatil imad
89:8 Allatee lam yukhlaq mithluha filbilad
89:9 Wathamood-allatheena jaboo ssakhra bilwad
89:10 Wafir'awna thil-awtad
89:11 Allatheena taghaw filbilad
89:12 Fa'aktharoo feeh-alfasad
89:13 Fasabba 'alayhim rabbuka sawta 'athab
89:14 Inna rabbaka labilmirsad
89:15 Fa 'ammal-insanu itha mabtalahu rabbuhu fa 'akramahu wana'amahu fayaqoolu rabbee akraman
89:16 Wa' amma itha mabtalahu faqadara 'alayhi rizqahu fayaqoolu rabbee ahanan
89:17 Kalla bal la tukrimoon-alyateem
89:18 Wala tahaddoona 'ala ta'am-ilmiskeen
89:19 Wata'kuloon-atturatha aklal lamma
89:20 Watuhibboon-almala hubban jamman
89:21 Kalla itha dukkat-il'ardu dakkan dakka
89:22 Waja'a rabbuka walmalaku saffan saffa
89:23 Wajee'a yawma-ithim bijahannama yawma-ithiy yatathakkar-ul-insanu wa'anna lahu-ththikra
89:24 Yaqoolu ya laytanee qaddamtu lihayatee
89:25 Fayawma-ithil la yu'aththibu 'athabahu ahad
89:26 Wala yoothiqu wathaqahu ahad
89:27 Ya ayyatuha-nnafs-ul-mutma'innah
89:28 Irji'ee ila rabbiki radiyatam mardiyyah
89:29 Fadkhulee fee 'ibadee
89:30 Wadkhulee jannatee

UNIT B

FAITH IN ACTION: THE STORY OF PROPHET IBRAHEEM

Ibraheem Searches For Allah

Questions?

1. Why was Prophet Ibraheem searching for Allah?
2. Where did he look first?
3. What did he finally learn about Allah?

Main Idea: We will follow Prophet Ibraheem's journey toward finding the One True God, Allah, our Creator.

Word Watch

| Worship | عبادة |
| Al-Hadi | الهادي |

This is a story for you to learn and enjoy. It is about a prophet who was searching to find the One True God.

Do you know this prophet's name?
It is Prophet Ibraheem عليه السلام .

The story begins thousands of years ago. Allah ﷻ tells us that ever since Prophet Ibraheem عليه السلام was a boy, he was always trying to find God.

Zaid: Why was Prophet Ibraheem searching so hard for Allah?

Dad: He was searching because:

People cannot have peace in their heart without knowing God and worshipping Him.

Every human being is supposed to look for the truth about God and believe in Him.

Searching in the Sky

One night, Ibraheem saw a star up in the sky. It was bright and beautiful. He thought he had found God. "That is my God," he said. Soon, the star disappeared. Ibraheem was disappointed. He said, " I will not worship gods that fade away!"

Prophet Ibraheem عليه السلام continued looking for God. He did not give up. He knew that good people must keep looking for the truth until they find it. Later, he saw the moon coming up. It was bright and beautiful. He got excited and said, "That must be God." But the same thing that had happened with the star happened with the moon. Slowly, the moon faded. By the morning, Ibraheem could barely see it. And by the afternoon, it had completely vanished.

Ibraheem thought, "If God does not show me the way, I will be among those people who are going on the wrong path."

Ibraheem looked again above him, where he saw the bright after-noon sun filling the sky with its bright glow.

Prophet Ibraheem عليه السلام was extremely happy.

Finally, he was sure that he had really found God. In his excite-ment, Ibraheem said: " That is my God. That is the greatest of all."

But like all days, this day came to an end. And as the time passed, the sun began to set. After a short while, the sun had completely set and the world had sunk into a deep darkness.

Allah is God

Prophet Ibraheem عليه السلام now knew the truth. The One God he was looking for could not be seen. That God was the Creator of the whole world. He created everything: the sun, the moon, the stars, and everything else.

Ibraheem عليه السلام felt good about what he had discovered. He told his people that he was not going to worship planets, idols, or statues. They were all false gods.

Ibraheem told them, "They are not my Gods. They did not create me. Allah created me. They do not feed me when I am hungry; Allah does. They do not cure me when I am sick; Allah does. I will only worship the one who created the Heavens, the Earth, and me. I will not associate any partners with Him, nor will I worship any other God. He cannot be seen, but He watches over us wherever we are."

"Ibraheem عليه السلام shared his thoughts with his people to teach faith in Allah, the One Creator. He said to them, "We need Allah's Guidance."

healthy habit

Always look for the truth, and follow it.

سورة الأنعام

Al-Anaam 6:75-79

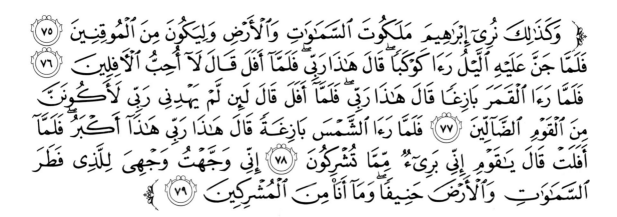

TRANSLITERATION

[75] Wakathalika nuree ibraheema malakoot-as-samawati wa al-'ardi waliyakoona min-al-mooqineen

[76] Falamma janna 'alayhi-llaylu ra'a kawkaban qala hatha rabbee, falamma afala qala la ohibb-ul-'aafileen

[77] Falamma ra'a-lqamara bazighan qala hatha rabbee falamma 'afala qala la-il lam yahdinee rabbee la'akoonanna min-al-qawm-id-dalleen

[78] Falamma ra'a-sh-shamsa bazighatan qala hatha rabbee hatha akbar falamma 'afalat qala ya qawmi innee baree'on mimma tushrikoon

[79] Innee wajjahtu wajhiya lillathee fatar-assamawati wal-arda haneefaw wama ana min-almushrikeen

MEANING TRANSLATION

Thus We showed Ibrahim the kingdom of the heavens and the earth, so that he might be firm in belief. (75) So, when the night enveloped him, he saw a star. He said, "This is my Lord." But, when it vanished, he said, "I do not like those who vanish." (76) Later, when he saw the moon rising, he said, "This is my Lord." But, when it vanished, he said, "Had my Lord not guided me, I would have been among those gone astray." (77) Thereafter, when he saw the sun rising, he said, "This is my Lord. This is greater." Again, when it vanished, he said, "O my people, I disown whatever you associate with Allah. (78) I have, indeed, turned my face straight towards the One who created the heavens and the earth, and I am not one of those who associate partners with Allah." (79)

Allah Guides Ibraheem

Allah loves those who look for the truth. He guides people who are eager to know and worship Him. So God, the Creator of the universe, helped Ibraheem عليه السلام and guided his heart to believe in Him. Ibraheem became happy and finally felt peace in his heart. He knew deep inside that Allah سبحانه وتعالى was his Only God, and he insisted on worshiping Him alone. Ibraheem عليه السلام realized that Allah is not like people, things, or the creatures that we see around us. He learned that Allah could not be seen in this life. Although Ibraheem عليه السلام could not see God, he knew that Allah سبحانه وتعالى could always see and hear him.

Allah is always there for us whenever we need help.

Ibraheem and the Birds

One Day, Ibraheem عليه السلام wanted to be sure that he was worshipping the One and Only True God. He went to the mountains and made a special du'aa.

He said: "Oh Lord, show me how you give life to the dead."

Allah asked Ibraheem: "Don't you believe?"

"Yes, I do, but I want my heart to be very sure," Ibraheem politely replied.

So, Allah ordered Ibraheem to do something unusual. He said: "Take four birds." He then instructed Ibraheem to kill them, cut them into pieces, and divide them into four sections. Then, Ibraheem was told to put each part on a different hill. Now Allah ordered Ibraheem to call the dead birds to come to him. Ibraheem obeyed Allah.

What do you think happened?
Do you think the dead birds came back to life?

Ibraheem was very anxious to see what would happen. He called the birds and immediately the pieces of each bird came together and the birds came back to life. In a few seconds the birds were hopping around Ibraheem.
Prophet Ibraheem was completely amazed. He thanked Allah, and he decided to call people to believe in Allah alone, and not to worship anyone or anything besides Allah.

سورة البقرة

Al-Baqara 2: 260

بِسْمِ اللّٰهِ الرَّحْمٰنِ الرَّحِيمِ

وَإِذْ قَالَ إِبْرَاهِيمُ رَبِّ أَرِنِي كَيْفَ تُحْىِ الْمَوْتَىٰ قَالَ أَوَلَمْ تُؤْمِنْ قَالَ بَلَىٰ وَلَٰكِن لِّيَطْمَئِنَّ قَلْبِي قَالَ فَخُذْ أَرْبَعَةً مِّنَ الطَّيْرِ فَصُرْهُنَّ إِلَيْكَ ثُمَّ اجْعَلْ عَلَىٰ كُلِّ جَبَلٍ مِّنْهُنَّ جُزْءًا ثُمَّ ادْعُهُنَّ يَأْتِينَكَ سَعْيًا وَاعْلَمْ أَنَّ اللّٰهَ عَزِيزٌ حَكِيمٌ ﴿٢٦٠﴾

TRANSLITERATION

[260] Wa-i th qala ibr aheemu rabbi arinee kayfa tuhyee - lmawta qala 'awalam tu'min qala bala walakin liyatma'inna qalbee, q ala fakhuth arba'atan min-at-tayri fasurhunna ilayka thumm-aj-'al 'ala kulli jabalim-minhunna juz'a, thumma od'uhunna ya'teenaka sa'yaw-wa'lam ann-Allaha 'azeezun hakeem

MEANING TRANSLATION

Remember when Ibrahim said: "My Lord, show me how You give life to the dead." He said: "Is it that you do not believe?" He said: "Of course, I do, but it is just to make my heart at peace." He said: "Then take four birds and tame them to your call, then put on every mountain a part from them, then give them a call, and they shall come to you rushing, and know that Allah is Mighty, Wise." (260)

Allah (is) Al-Hadi

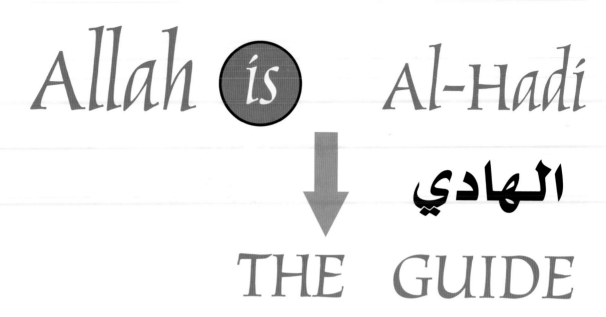

الهادي

THE GUIDE

Allah guides hearts to the truth, and to what is good for people in this life and the next.

healthy habit

Always pray to Allah to guide you to the truth, and to obey and worship Him.

 time

Plant some seeds in a container. Give them water until they grow green. Then ask yourself: Who gave them life and made them after they were dry like tiny rocks?

Thinking Critically

1. Why can't the sun, the moon, and the planets be God?
2. Why is it important to find out who God is?

Study  Questions

1 Why did Ibraheem search for Allah?

2 Where did Ibraheem look for Allah?

3 What was the first thing Ibraheem thought was God? What did he think after that?

4 Can we see Allah in this life? Why?

5 Why did Ibraheem ask Allah to show him a sign?

6 What did Allah tell Ibraheem to do?

7 What happened to the birds?

Prophet Ibraheem: Iman Made Him Brave

Questions?

1. Can a human being be God?
2. Who was Num-rude? Why were people afraid of him?
3. What did Ibraheem do to prove to the people that their idols were not God?
4. Why wasn't Ibraheem afraid of the king?

Main Idea: Allah is the true God and Creator of the universe. Prophet Ibraheem عليه السلام was brave and spoke the truth about God. He told everyone that idols cannot be gods.

Word Watch

Temple	مَعبَد
King Num-rude	الملك نَمْرود
Al-Haqq	الحق

Babylon in Iraq

Ibraheem lived in a country called Iraq. The ruler of Iraq was a very rude and unjust king. His name was Num-rude.

Num-rude was a king who thought of himself as God. He wanted his people to worship him and his idols made of stone. Num-rude did not care what the people thought about these gods. He just insisted that the people obey his orders. The people knew that Num-rude was mean and unjust; they were scared of him. So they worshipped the idols without objecting.

In the streets of Babylon, a city in Iraq, the people bought and sold idols. One of the most famous carpenters in the city sold idols that he made out of wood and stone. This carpenter had a son named Ibraheem.

Unlike the rest of the people, Ibraheem was a brave boy and was not afraid of King Num-rude. Prophet Ibraheem knew that these idols were not gods, but as a child he could do nothing.

B15

Anyone who spoke against the idols was punished. Prophet Ibraheem عليه السلام was not afraid of the punishment. Speaking the truth was important to him. He refused to worship the idols, and he decided to tell everyone not to worship them either.

Speaking the truth took a great deal of courage. Ibraheem told the people that Allah was the Greatest. And only He could benefit or harm them. He reminded them that Allah is All-Seeing and All-Knowing.

Prophet Ibraheem called his father and other people to worship Allah, their creator. But it was no use. No one listened to him. They thought that King Num-rude and their idols were gods.

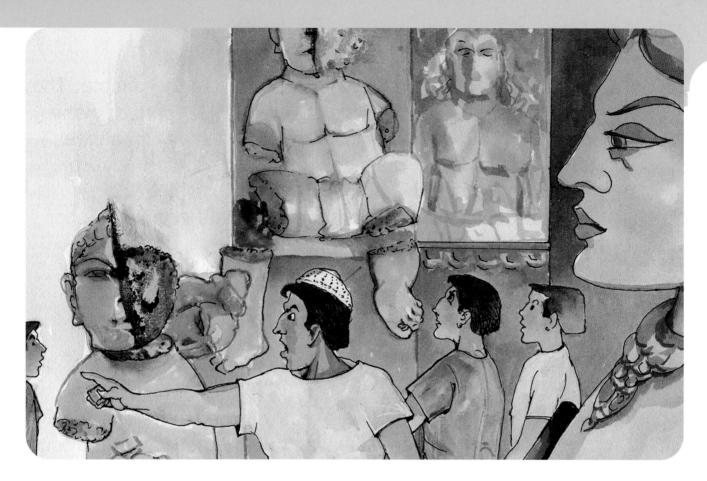

Poor Idols

Prophet Ibraheem decided to prove that the idols could do nothing, and that worshipping them was a big mistake.

One day, Prophet Ibraheem went to the temple where people worshipped idols. When nobody was around, he used an axe to smash the idols. He destroyed all of the idols except for the largest one. He then placed the axe by the largest idol and left the temple.

The next day, when people went to their temple, they were shocked and upset at what they saw. They shouted with anger, "Who has done this to our gods? He must be an evil man!"

A few people said, " We heard a youth speak badly of them. He is called Ibraheem."

They brought Prophet Ibraheem عليه السلام to the temple. They asked him if he had smashed their gods. He replied, "Why don't you ask them (the idols), and see if they can answer."

The people said, " You know that our gods do not speak."

Prophet Ibraheem عليه السلام then asked:

" How do you worship gods who can neither help you nor harm you? Why do you not worship Allah ﷻ ?"

The people were silent because they knew he was right. But they could not stand to hear him talk.

What did we learn from this?

1. We should be brave and tell the truth no matter whom we are speaking to, whether it is one of our family members, or the king of a country. We should be polite, however.

2. If we tell the truth, then we have nothing to fear.

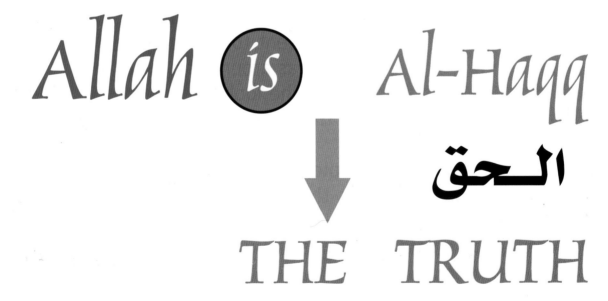

That is because Allah is the only Real One and what they invoke other than Him is false... (30) Luqman 31: 30

Thinking Critically

Write two paragraphs about the following:

Did you ever have to tell the truth in a tough situation? Was it hard? What happened? Why is telling the truth the best choice?

healthy
h a b i t

Always look for the truth. If someone says that you are wrong, do not get upset. Ask about the right way and follow it.

Study  Questions

1. Who was the king of Iraq? What did he want his people to do?

2. Who was Ibraheem عليه السلام ? Who was his father?

3. Why did Ibraheem عليه السلام not like idols?

4. What courageous act did Prophet Ibraheem عليه السلام do to prove to his people that worshipping idols is a mistake?

5. What was the people's reaction when they saw the idols smashed?

When Fire Does Not Burn!

Questions?

1 Can anyone harm you if Allah does not allow this?
2 How did King Num-rude plan to kill Ibraheem عليه السلام ?
3 What happened to Ibraheem?

Main Idea: The story of Prophet Ibraheem shows us that Allah tests the faithful. Sometimes they are saved in this life from harm, and sometimes they suffer. Allah chose to save Ibraheem from King Num-rude and his fire.

Word Watch

Al-Hafeeth   الحفيظ

The people of Iraq went to King Num-rude. One person said, "He smashed our idols."

Another one said, "He mocked them."

"And he refused to call you God," said the third. The king's face turned red.

King Num-rude ordered his soldiers to find Prophet Ibraheem. Prophet Ibraheem عليه السلام was brought to the king. He was not worried or afraid. He عليه السلام had great trust in Allah سبحانه وتعالى , and he feared no one except Him.

"You smashed our idols, and you refused to worship me," said King Num-rude.

Prophet Ibraheem told him about Allah سبحانه وتعالى . "My Lord created me and He guides me. He gives me food and drink. When I am ill, He cures me. He is the Only One who can make me die and then bring me back to life."

" I can do the same: I can make people die and make them live," said King Num-rude. He ordered his guards to bring two people from the prison. Both were criminals and deserved to die. He ordered one person to be killed and the other one to be freed.

"You see, I can do that. I can kill or save," Num-rude said.

Prophet Ibraheem was upset about what Num-rude had done, so he replied, "Allah can bring the sun from the east. So, make it rise from the west." King Num-rude could not respond. He became very furious. He couldn't believe that Ibraheem عليه السلام dared to speak to him like that!

King Num-rude ordered Prophet Ibraheem عليه السلام to be jailed. That did not make Prophet Ibraheem عليه السلام change his mind.

King Num-rude then ordered his soldiers to burn Ibraheem alive. The non-believers gathered an enormous amount of firewood and made a very big fire. Even birds who flew over it got burned. The non-believers tied Prophet Ibraheem's عليه السلام legs and hands and threw him into the fire. They were excited to watch him get burned.

But to their surprise, he was not burned.

Prophet Ibraheem عليه السلام made du'aa' to Allah ﷻ and asked Allah for help. Allah ﷻ ordered the fire not to burn Ibraheem. "O Fire! be cool and safe for Ibraheem," Allah ordered. And the unbelievers were surprised to see Prophet Ibraheem عليه السلام unharmed.

After this, some people believed in Prophet Ibraheem عليه السلام and moved with him to a place called Palestine.

WORDS OF WISDOM
Holy Qura'n

سورة البقرة

Al-Baqara 2: 258

بِسْمِ اللَّهِ الرَّحْمَٰنِ الرَّحِيمِ

أَلَمْ تَرَ إِلَى الَّذِى حَاجَّ إِبْرَٰهِمَ فِى رَبِّهِ أَنْ ءَاتَىٰهُ اللَّهُ الْمُلْكَ إِذْ قَالَ إِبْرَٰهِمُ رَبِّيَ الَّذِى يُحْىِ وَيُمِيتُ قَالَ أَنَا۠ أُحْىِ وَأُمِيتُ قَالَ إِبْرَٰهِمُ فَإِنَّ اللَّهَ يَأْتِى بِالشَّمْسِ مِنَ الْمَشْرِقِ فَأْتِ بِهَا مِنَ الْمَغْرِبِ فَبُهِتَ الَّذِى كَفَرَ وَاللَّهُ لَا يَهْدِى الْقَوْمَ الظَّٰلِمِينَ ﴿٢٥٨﴾

TRANSLITERATION

[258] Alam tara ilal-lathee hajja ibraheema fee rabbihi an atahu-llahul-mulk, ith qala ibraheemu rabbiy -allathee yuhyee wayumeet, qala ana 'uhyee wa'umeet, qala ibraheemu fa-'inn Allaha ya'tee bishshamsi min-almashriqi fa'ti biha min almaghrib, fabuhit allathee kafar, wallahu la yahdil-qawm-ath-thalimeen.

MEANING TRANSLATION

Do you not know the one who argued with Ibrahim about his Lord, because Allah had given him kingship? When Ibrahim said: "My Lord is the One Who gives life and brings death," he said: "I give life and I bring death." Said Ibrahim: "Allah brings the sun out from the East; now, you bring it out from the West." Here, baffled was the one who disbelieved, and Allah does not bring the wrongdoers to the right path. (258)

1 Those who love Allah ﷻ have strong trust in Him.

2 They are courageous, and they do not fear people. They only fear and worship Allah ﷻ .

3 Allah ﷻ will test the believers to make their faith stronger. Sometimes He saves them from harm like Prophet Ibraheem. Other times, believers might suffer. They will win *Jannah*.

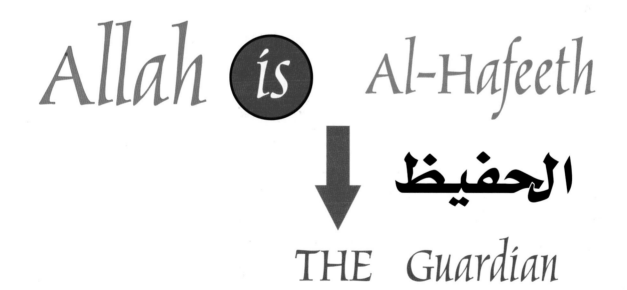

Allah **is** Al-Hafeeth

الحفيظ

THE Guardian

"Allah is the best Guardian, and He is the Most Merciful of all."

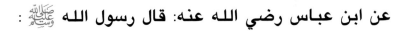

WORDS OF WISDOM
Hadeeth Shareef

حديث شريف

Narrated By Tirmithi

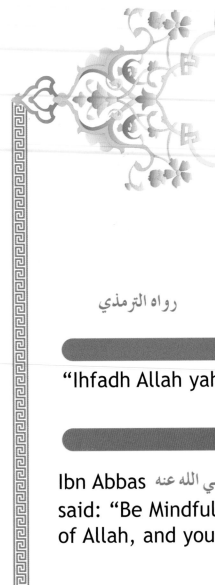

عن ابن عباس رضي الله عنه: قال رسول الله ﷺ :

"اِحْفَظِ اللّهَ يَحْفَظْكَ، اِحْفَظِ اللّهَ تَجِدْهُ تُجَاهَكَ."

رواه الترمذي

TRANSLITERATION

"Ihfadh Allah yahfadhk, ihfadh Allah tajidhu tujahak."

MEANING TRANSLATION

Ibn Abbas رضي الله عنه reported that the Prophet Muhammad ﷺ said: "Be Mindful of Allah, and He will guard you. Be mindful of Allah, and you will find Him supporting you."

ACTIVITY time

Get into groups and create acrostics for the word "faith" or "faithful." This means that you supply a poetic line for each letter in the word "faith" or "faithful." Share your poems or acrostics with the class and collect them into a Little Book of Faith.

Study  Questions

1 How did king Num-rude find out about Prophet Ibraheem?

2 What did Prophet Ibraheem say to Num-rude?

3 What punishment did Num-rude give to Prophet Ibraheem at first? Did Prophet Ibraheem عليه السلام change his mind?

4 What was the last punishment Num-rude ordered for Prophet Ibraheem? Did Prophet Ibraheem عليه السلام change his mind the second time?

5 Did Prophet Ibraheem عليه السلام have weak or strong faith, and did he and trust in Allah? How did Allah ﷻ reward him?

Prophet Ibraheem Travels to Makkah

Questions?

1 Where is Makkah?
2 Who was the first son of Prophet Ibraheem?
3 Who was Ismaeel's mother?
4 Why did Ibraheem take his family to Makkah?
5 Have you ever tasted Zamzam water? Where does this water come from?

Main Idea: Allah ﷻ loved Ibraheem, so He tested him often. He gave him great rewards as he passed each test. In this test Ibraheem was ordered to leave his wife and baby in the desert. He obeyed.

Word Watch

Isma'eel	إسماعيل
As-Safa	الصَّفا
Al-Marwah	المَروة
Zamzam	زمـزم
Ar-Razzaq	الرَّزاق
Hager	هاجر

Prophet Ibraheem عليه السلام and his wife **Hager** had no children for a very long time. When Allah سبحانه وتعالى blessed him with a child, Prophet Ibraheem was very happy. He named the child **Isma'eel**. This means, "God listens to the prayer." Isma'eel was Allah's reward for Prophet Ibraheem's faith and patience.

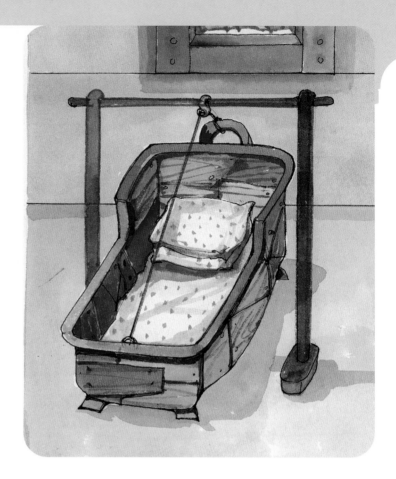

Prophet Ibraheem's عليه السلام happiness did not last long. Shortly after Isma'eel was born, Allah gave Ibraheem another test. God ordered Ibraheem to take his wife Hager and their only son Isma'eel to Makkah and leave them there. Makkah was far away in the hot desert of Arabia, and they had no water or food at that time. Prophet Ibraheem عليه السلام obeyed Allah's command without hesitation.

How hard do you think this test must have been for Prophet Ibraheem عليه السلام , his wife, and his son?

Ibraheem عليه السلام traveled with Hager and Isma'eel to Makkah. No one lived there at that time. Makkah was a place with no people, no houses, no trees, and no food or water. Ibraheem took his family there and prepared to leave them. His wife Hager asked him, "Who will take care of us here after you leave?"

"Allah," Ibraheem answered. His answer reassured Hager. "Then Allah will not abandon us," Hager said.

Ibraheem made a du'aa' to Allah to protect and take care of Hager and Isma'eel.

سورة إبراهيم

Surah Ibrahim 14: 37

رَبَّنَآ إِنِّى أَسْكَنتُ مِن ذُرِّيَّتِى بِوَادٍ غَيْرِ ذِى زَرْعٍ عِندَ بَيْتِكَ ٱلْمُحَرَّمِ رَبَّنَا لِيُقِيمُوا۟ ٱلصَّلَوٰةَ فَٱجْعَلْ أَفْـِٔدَةً مِّنَ ٱلنَّاسِ تَهْوِىٓ إِلَيْهِمْ وَٱرْزُقْهُم مِّنَ ٱلثَّمَرَٰتِ لَعَلَّهُمْ يَشْكُرُونَ ﴿٣٧﴾

TRANSLITERATION

Rabbana innee askantu min thurriyyatee biwadin ghayri thee zar'in 'inda baytik almuharram, rabbana liyuqeemo-ssalata faij'al af'idatam min annasi tahwee ilayhim, waorzuqhum min ath-thamarati la'allahum yashkuroon

MEANING TRANSLATION

Our Lord, I have settled some of my children in a valley of no vegetation, close to Your sanctified House, so that, Our Lord, they may establish Salah. So, make hearts of people yearn towards them, and provide them with fruits, so that they may be grateful. (37)

After a few days, Hager and Isma'eel used up what little food they had. They were left with nothing. Hager became very worried about her baby. She had to find something to eat or drink so Isma'eel could feed on her milk. She looked around but found no help.

She went up to a nearby hill that is now called "As-Safa." She climbed up to look for anybody who could help her, but sadly, she saw nothing. Then she ran to another hill about half a mile away. That hill is now called "Al-Marwah." She went up on Al-Marwah and looked around, but again she found nothing. She did not give up, but ran back to As-Safa. She ran between As-Safa and Al-Marwah seven times, but she found no food, water, or help.

Although Hager trusted that Allah would take care of her, she did not sit back and wait for a miracle. She did her best to find food and water for herself and her baby. By the time she was finished searching, Hager was thirsty and exhausted. She decided to go back to her son Isma'eel. As she got close to Isma'eel, she was surprised by what she saw.

What do you think she found?

Hager saw a spring of water coming up near the baby's feet. She could not believe her eyes. Hager carried Isma'eel and gave him some water. She bathed him to cool him down. She then drank and refreshed herself. Later, she made a pond to keep the water there. The spring is now called Zamzam.

As-Safa

Al-Ka'bah

Zamzam

Al-Marwa

Muslims on the As-Safa Hill

Makkah
Now

Hager was so happy and grateful to Allah. She remembered Ibraheem's words before he left. He had said, "Allah will take care of you." She always trusted that Allah would never abandon her and Isma'eel. He had truly taken care of her. He had provided her with water and food when she most needed it. Some birds started to come to the pond, and life started to look much better.

Allah (is) Ar-Razzaq

الرزاق

THE Ever-Provider

He is the one who gives us rizq, like food, water, medicine and all the things we need.

Allah says:

﴿ وَكَأَيِّن مِّن دَآبَّةٍ لَّا تَحْمِلُ رِزْقَهَا ٱللَّهُ يَرْزُقُهَا وَإِيَّاكُمْ وَهُوَ ٱلسَّمِيعُ ٱلْعَلِيمُ ۝ ﴾

How many an animal there is that does not carry its provision. Allah gives provision to it as well as to you... (60)

Surah Al-Ankaboot 29: 60

Later, a traveling caravan that belonged to the Arabian tribe of Jurhum saw birds flying over Makkah.

"There must be food and water over there, because the birds are flying there!" one man said.

"There has never been water or food there before," another man said.

So they sent a group to look and see. The group found Hager and Isma'eel by the water. Then the whole caravan came, and the people asked her for permission to get some water. Hager was a very kind lady. She allowed them to use the water and set up homes nearby. They gave her food and kept her company. This was the start of the city we now call Makkah.

When Isma'eel grew up, he married a young lady from the tribe of Jurhum.

WORDS OF WISDOM
Hadeeth Shareef

حديث شريف

Narrated By Tirmithi

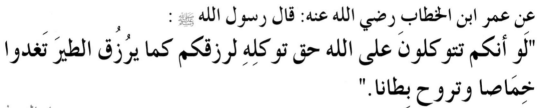

عن عمر ابن الخطاب رضي الله عنه: قال رسول الله ﷺ :
"لَو أنكم تتوكلونَ على الله حق توكلهِ لرزقكم كما يرُزُق الطيرَ تَغدوا خِمَاصا وتروح بِطانا."

رواه الترمذي

TRANSLITERATION

"Law annakum tat-wakkaloona alallahi haqqa tawakkulihi larazaqkum kama yarzuqu-ttayra, taghdo khimasan wa taroohu bitana"

MEANING TRANSLATION

Omar ibn Al-Khattab رضي الله عنه reporated that the Prophet ﷺ said: "If you truly rely on Allah, He will provide for you as He provides for birds. They leave [the nest] hungry in the morning and return full in the evening."

Think Critically:

In what ways was Isma'eel a special child?

healthy
h a b i t

Always have full trust in Allah. Always rely on your Creator. However, do your part by working hard, just like Hager, the mother of Isma'eel.

Study  Questions

1   Where did Prophet Ibraheem take his wife and son? Why?

2   What are the names of his wife and son?

3   How could Ibraheem leave his wife and son in the hot, empty desert?

4   What did Ibraheem's wife do when she ran out of food?

5   How did Ibraheem's family survive?

6   What are the names of the two hills that Hager ran between in the story?

7   Write three lessons we learn from this story?

The Hardest Test

Questions?

1. What did Allah ask Prophet Ibraheem to do?
2. Why was this the most difficult test for Ibraheem?
3. What did Isma'eel say when his father told him about the vision he saw?
4. Did Prophet Ibraheem obey Allah?

Main Idea: Allah ﷻ sometimes tests us to see if we truly love and trust Him. If we pass the tests by obeying Allah, He will be pleased, and we will win great rewards in this life and the next life.

Word Watch

| Khaleel-ullah | خليل الله |

Prophet Ibraheem's Vision

The test began when Prophet Ibraheem عليه السلام had a vision. A vision is like a dream, but Prophet Ibraheem's vision was a true message from Allah. In his vision, Prophet Ibraheem saw that Allah سبحانه وتعالى wanted him to sacrifice his only son, Ismaeel. Can you imagine that?

How could Prophet Ibraheem take his beloved son, the joy that he had waited so long to have, hold him down, and kill him? Prophet Ibraheem probably wished that he had not seen the vision. Prophet Ibraheem had always obeyed Allah's commands in the past, but this time the test was much harder.

How hard do you think this test must have been for Prophet Ibraheem, his wife, and his son?

Prophet Ibraheem had to choose between his love for Allah, which was very strong, and his love for his son, which was also strong. He did not want to hurt his only son Ismaeel, but he also knew that he had to obey Allah.

What do you think Prophet Ibraheem عليه السلام should decide? Why?

For some time, Prophet Ibraheem doubted his vision. But he saw the vision again and again. After seeing the vision for the third time, Ibraheem knew that he had to obey Allah's command.

Think about it!

Can you imagine what Prophet Ibraheem must have been feeling?

Do you think his decision was easy to make?

Can you think of some questions Prophet Ibraheem must have asked himself?

Isma'eel Obeys Allah and His Father

Now Prophet Ibraheem عليه السلام had to tell Ismaeel about the vision.

What do you think Ismaeel عليه السلام said?

Let us see what happened.
Prophet Ibraheem عليه السلام said to Ismaeel عليه السلام :

﴿ فَلَمَّا بَلَغَ مَعَهُ ٱلسَّعْىَ قَالَ يَٰبُنَىَّ إِنِّىٓ أَرَىٰ فِى ٱلْمَنَامِ أَنِّىٓ أَذْبَحُكَ فَٱنظُرْ مَاذَا تَرَىٰ ﴾

... "O my little son, I have seen in a dream that I am slaughtering you, so consider, what is your opinion?"... (102) Surah As-Saafat 37: 102

Prophet Ismaeel عليه السلام could have kept silent or told Prophet Ibraheem عليه السلام not to kill him. He could have cried or just run away. But, Prophet Ismaeel عليه السلام also had strong faith and trust in Allah ﷻ. He tried to comfort his father, saying:

﴿ قَالَ يَٰٓأَبَتِ ٱفْعَلْ مَا تُؤْمَرُ سَتَجِدُنِىٓ إِن شَآءَ ٱللَّهُ مِنَ ٱلصَّٰبِرِينَ ۝ ﴾

... "O my dear father, do what you have been ordered to do. You will find me, insha'allah , (if Allah wills) one of those who endure patiently." (102) Surah As-Saafat 37: 102

Subhan Allah! Prophet Ismaeel believed so strongly in Allah that he knew following His commands would never be wrong, even if that meant giving up his life. He encouraged his father to do the right thing, and they were both rewarded.

Ismaeel's answer gave Prophet Ibraheem strength. Prophet Ibraheem took Ismaeel to the place of sacrifice. Of course, Prophet Ibraheem was suffering every step of the way.

Iblees Tries to Stop Ibraheem

Iblees was disappointed to see Ibraheem عليه السلام and Ismaeel عليه السلام following Allah's orders, so he tried to stop them. Iblees wanted Prophet Ibraheem عليه السلام to disobey Allah. He planned to trick Ibraheem as he did to Prophet Adam before. So he appeared three times in Mina, a place near Makkah, and tried to convince Prophet Ibraheem to disobey Allah. He gave him all kinds of reasons not to sacrifice his son.

Prophet Ibraheem did not listen to the Shaytan and knew that he had to follow Allah's orders no matter what. Each time Iblees appeared, Prophet Ibraheem threw rocks at him to make him go away. That is why when Muslims go to Hajj, they throw pebbles at the places where Shaytan appeared to Prophet Ibraheem in Mina.

Prophet Ibraheem laid Prophet Ismaeel on the ground. He made him face away from him because he could not bear to look at his son's face in this situation. A moment before Ibraheem sacrificed his son, Allah sent down a ram to be sacrificed in place of Isma'eel. He also sent this verse down to Prophet Ibraheem:

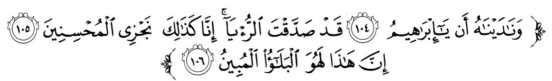

..."O Ibrahim, (104) You did make the dream come true." This is how We reward those who are good in their deeds. (105) This was indeed a trial that clearly demonstrated (their obedience). (106) Surah As-Saafat 37: 104-106

Let us say together:

Allah-u-Akbar! Allah-u-Akbar! Allah-u-Akbar!

Ibraheem: Khaleel-ullah

And so, by obeying Allah and passing the hardest test, Prophet Ibraheem عليه السلام won everything. He got his son back, he won the love of Allah سبحانه وتعالى , and the love and respect of his only son, Prophet Isma'eel. He also won the love of many people for all time.

Allah chose Prophet Ibraheem to be His beloved friend, and called him " **Khaleel-ullah,**" which means, "beloved friend of Allah."

Here are some more verses about Prophet Ibraheem in the Qur'an:

﴿ إِنَّ إِبْرَاهِيمَ كَانَ أُمَّةً قَانِتًا لِّلَّهِ حَنِيفًا وَلَمْ يَكُ مِنَ الْمُشْرِكِينَ ﴾

Surely, Ibrahim was an Ummah (a whole community in himself), devoted to Allah, a man of pure faith; and he was not among the Mushriks (i.e. those who associate partners with Allah) (120)
Surah An-Nahl 16: 120

Today, we also call Prophet Ibraheem the "Father of the Prophets." Do you know why?

B43

Lessons Learned

❶ In this life I will have many tests from Allah ﷻ , and my faith and trust in Allah will always be tested.

❷ The love of Allah should be more than the love for anyone else, even children or family.

❸ If I choose the love of Allah, I will gain rewards, and I will lose nothing.

❹ I should obey my parents, even if they ask me to do hard things.

❺ Iblees will try hard always to make me disobey Allah, especially at times when I feel tired, weak, or afraid.

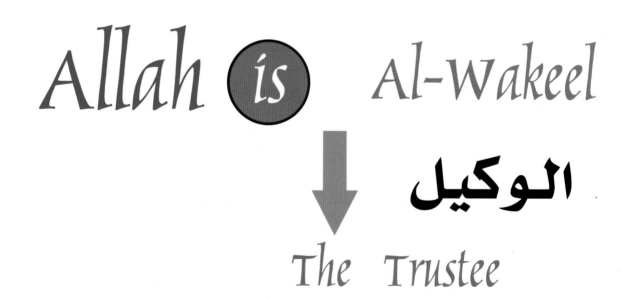

Allah (is) Al-Wakeel

الوكيل

The Trustee

...In Allah the believers should place their trust. (160)
Surah Al-E-Imran 3: 160

Think Critically:

❶ Why did Allah ﷾ tell us this story in the Qur'an?

❷ What makes Prophet Ibraheem's story so important for Muslims?

❸ Why do you think we need to hear it?

Study  Questions

❶ Why was Prophet Ismaeel عليه السلام very special to Prophet Ibraheem عليه السلام ?

❷ What were some of the tests that Prophet Ibraheem went through in his life?

❸ Why was sacrificing Prophet Ismaeel the hardest test for Prophet Ibraheem?

❹ What made Prophet Ismaeel obey his father?

❺ How did Allah save Prophet Ismaeel? How did Allah reward Prophet Ibraheem? give two ways.

❻ Why do Muslims visit the city of Mina during the Hajj?

Building Al-Ka'bah

Questions?

❶ What is Al-Ka'bah?
❷ Who built Al-Ka'bah?
❸ Why was it built?

Main Idea: Learn how Al-Ka'bah was built, and why it is the holiest place for Muslims.

Word Watch

Al-Ka'bah	الكعبة
Al-Hajar-ul-Aswad	الحجر الأسود
Maqamu Ibraheem	مقامُ إبراهيم
Al-Hajj	الحج

Prophet Ibraheem عليه السلام received a very important order from Allah. He was ordered to go to Makkah again and build a masjid. This was the first House of Allah to be built on Earth.

Ibraheem عليه السلام traveled again from Palestine to Makkah. He told Isma'eel عليه السلام about this great project. It is a great honor for anyone to build a masjid. Isma'eel عليه السلام was very excited to help his dear father in this great project.

Ibraheem عليه السلام and Isma'eel عليه السلام collected big stones from the mountains nearby. They dug in the Earth to make the house stand strong and firm. They cut and piled the stones very well. They also placed a special stone to mark the southeast corner of the house. It was the place of **Al-Hajar-ul-Aswad,** or the Black Stone. It was a white stone that came from *Jannah*. Later, the white stone became black because of the many sins people committed.

Prophets Ibraheem and Isma'eel built the four walls of the masjid, row by row. Ibraheem made the building look like a big cube. That is why it is called **Al-Ka'bah.**

Al—Ka'bah means "the Cube Building". The walls rose higher and higher. Isma'eel brought a large rock for his father to stand on and reach higher.

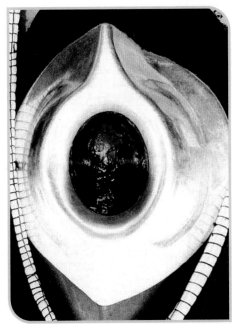

Prophet Ibraheem السلام عليه stood on the rock to build the top rows of the walls. This rock is still in Makkah, near Al-Ka'bah; visitors can see the footprints of Prophet Ibraheem on it.

While Ibraheem and Isma'eel were building Al-Ka'ba, they would take a break to rest. During the break, they would walk around the building to see how it looked. They would also say beautiful prayers. They prayed to Allah to accept their work, and to make them and their children good Muslims.

They prayed to Allah to teach them how to perform their worship. They also asked Allah to send to people after them a messenger to teach them Allah's Book and wisdom, so they would become good people.

Allah answered Ibraheem's prayers. Allah made one of the descendants of Isma'eel a great messenger.

Do you know who that messenger was?

That messenger was Prophet Muhammad

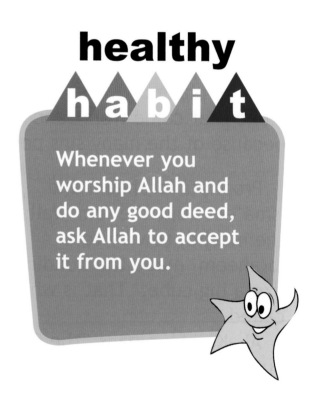

healthy
h a b i t

Whenever you worship Allah and do any good deed, ask Allah to accept it from you.

سورة البقرة

Surah Al-Baqara 2: 127-129

بِسْمِ ٱللَّهِ ٱلرَّحْمَٰنِ ٱلرَّحِيمِ

﴿ وَإِذْ يَرْفَعُ إِبْرَٰهِۦمُ ٱلْقَوَاعِدَ مِنَ ٱلْبَيْتِ وَإِسْمَٰعِيلُ رَبَّنَا تَقَبَّلْ مِنَّآ إِنَّكَ أَنتَ ٱلسَّمِيعُ ٱلْعَلِيمُ ۝ رَبَّنَا وَٱجْعَلْنَا مُسْلِمَيْنِ لَكَ وَمِن ذُرِّيَّتِنَآ أُمَّةً مُّسْلِمَةً لَّكَ وَأَرِنَا مَنَاسِكَنَا وَتُبْ عَلَيْنَآ إِنَّكَ أَنتَ ٱلتَّوَّابُ ٱلرَّحِيمُ ۝ رَبَّنَا وَٱبْعَثْ فِيهِمْ رَسُولًا مِّنْهُمْ يَتْلُوا۟ عَلَيْهِمْ ءَايَٰتِكَ وَيُعَلِّمُهُمُ ٱلْكِتَٰبَ وَٱلْحِكْمَةَ وَيُزَكِّيهِمْ إِنَّكَ أَنتَ ٱلْعَزِيزُ ٱلْحَكِيمُ ۝ ﴾

TRANSLITERATION

[127] Wa-ith yarfa'u ibraheemu alqawa'ida mina albayti wa-ism a'eelu rabban ataqabbal minna innaka anta a lssamee'u al'aleemu

[128] Rabban awa ij'aln amuslimayni laka wamin thurriyy-atin aommatan muslimatan laka waarin aman asikan awatub 'alayn ainnaka anta a lttawwabu alrraheemu

[129] Rabban awa ib'ath feehim rasoolan minhum yatloo 'alayhim ayatika wayu'allimuhumu alkitaba wa alhikmata wayuzakkeehim innaka anta al'azeezu alhakeemu

MEANING TRANSLATION

When Ibrahim was raising up the foundations of the House, along with Isma'il (Ishmael) (supplicating): "Our Lord accept (this service) from us! Indeed, You - and You alone - are the All-Hearing, the All-Knowing! (127) Our Lord, make us both submissive to You, and (make) of our progeny as well, a people submissive to You and show us our ways of Pilgrimage and accept our repentance. Indeed, You - and You alone - are the Most-Relenting, the Very-Merciful. (128) And, our Lord, raise in their midst a Messenger from among them, who should recite to them Your verses, and teach them the Book and the wisdom, and cleanse them of all impurities. Indeed You, and You alone, are the All-Mighty, the All-Wise." (129)

The Call to Hajj

Ibraheem and Isma'eel completed building Al-Ka'bah. It became the holiest place for all Muslims. It was the first masjid built on Earth.

Allah ordered Ibraheem to do another thing. Allah wanted him to call all people to come and worship Allah in and around Al-Ka'bah once a year. Ibraheem asked Allah: "How can people hear me when they are so far away."

Allah told Ibraheem: "You make the call, and I will make them all hear it". Ibraheem stood by Al-Ka'bah and made the call for **Al-Hajj** الحج. Allah made all people hear the call of Ibraheem even without loudspeakers or phones. These things were not invented at that time. People started to come to Makkah to worship Allah once a year at Al-Ka'bah. The place where Ibraheem stood and made the first call for Hajj is called "Maqamu Ibraheem مقام إبراهيم," which means the station or standing place of Ibraheem. This was the beginning of Al-Hajj.

Study  Questions

1 Where was Al-Ka'bah built?

2 Who built Al-Ka'bah?

3 What is Al-Hajar-ul Aswad?

4 Why did Allah want Prophet Ibraheem to build Al-Ka'bah?

5 Which messenger is the descendant of Prophets Ibraheem and Isma'eel?

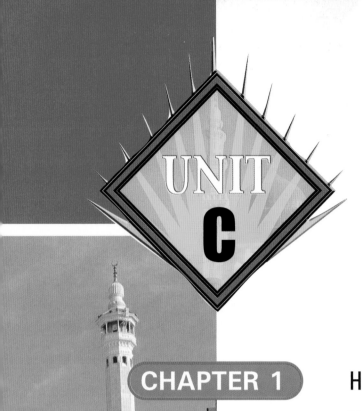

UNIT C

WORSHIPPING ALLAH

HAJJ: THE FIFTH PILLAR OF ISLAM

Questions?

① What is Hajj?
② How does a Muslim perform Hajj?
③ What is the wisdom behind the Hajj rituals?

Main Idea: Hajj is the fifth pillar of Islam.

LABBAYK ALLAHUMMA LABBAYK

Word  **Watch**

Hajj	حَـجّ
Thul Hijjah	ذو الـحِجة
Makkah	مكـة
Ihram	إحرام
Tawaf	طواف
Sa'iy	سعِي
Zamzam	زمزم
Mina	مِنى
Arafah	عرفات
Muzdalifah	مُزدلِفة
Jamrat	جَمرات

وَلِلّٰهِ عَلَى النَّاسِ حِجُّ الْبَيْتِ مَنِ اسْتَطَاعَ إِلَيْهِ سَبِيلًا ﴾

... it is obligatory on the people to perform Hajj of the House - on everyone who has the ability to manage (his) way to it... (97)

"People must make a pilgrimage to Allah's house (Al- Ka'bah) if they are able to travel to it."

Surah Al-E-Imran 3: 97

Story Time

Bilal and Sarah were so excited. They couldn't even sleep that night. Their parents were coming back from Hajj in Makkah the ne... day.

Bilal and Sarah stayed with their uncle and aunt while their parents were at Hajj.

WHAT IS "HAJJ"?

Hajj is **the fifth pillar** of Islam.   It is fard or compulsory on every adult Muslim, if he or she is in good health and can afford it. The hajj happens once a year in the lunar month of Thul Hijjah. This means, "the month of Hajj." It is the twelfth and last month of the lunar year.

During Hajj, people remember Allah by praying, making du'aa', and remembering Allah's blessings.

Bilal's Parents in Hajj

Every night, Bilal and Sarah sit with their uncle and aunt watching programs about Hajj on TV. "I wish I could see Mom and Dad," says Sarah.

"Me too," says her uncle, "but remember that there are more than two million Muslims there."

WHAT DID BILAL AND SARAH'S PARENTS DO FIRST?

Bilal and Sarah's parents finally came back, and everybody was waiting for them at the airport. The children jumped up and down when they saw their parents coming out of the plane. They ran to them and hugged them hard. At home, parents gave the children all the gifts they had brought from Makkah and Madinah. The children were so happy, they wanted their parents to tell them about everything they had done in Hajj. Mama told them that they were very tired and that they would tell them about Hajj the next morning, Insha Allah.

In the morning, all the family prayed Fajr together. Then the parents started to describe how they performed Hajj:

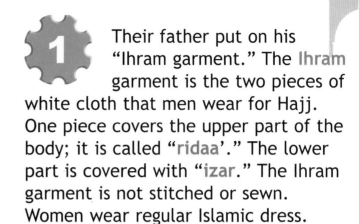

1 Their father put on his "Ihram garment." The Ihram garment is the two pieces of white cloth that men wear for Hajj. One piece covers the upper part of the body; it is called "ridaa'." The lower part is covered with "izar." The Ihram garment is not stitched or sewn. Women wear regular Islamic dress.

2 Both parents made "Ihram," which is the "niyyah," or intention, of doing Hajj for the sake of Allah. Then they said loudly, "Labbayk Alluhuma Labbayk, Labbayka la Shareeka laka labbayk."

3 They made "Tawaf," or circled Al-Ka'bah, seven times counter-clockwise. While doing that, they made du'aa' and thikr to Allah.

Al-Ka'bah is the first masjid, or House of Worship, built on Earth. As we learned earlier, Prophets Ibraheem and Isma'eel built it thousands of years ago when Allah ordered them to do so. Going around Al-Ka'bah teaches Muslims many lessons. One of the lessons is that they should stay close to the houses of Allah and worship Allah there continuously, seven days a week if they can.

4 Bilal and Sarah's parents made "Sa'iy." Sa'iy in Arabic means "walking fast." In Hajj, Muslims walk fast back and forth, seven times between two rocky hills called As-Safa and Al-Marwah. This reminds us of the time when Hager walked between these two hills looking for water for her infant son Isma'eel.

When Hager came back to him, she found water gushing out of the ground by his feet.

The Hujjaj (Hajj pilgrims) drink from that blessed water, which is called Zamzam water, which is still there near Al-Ka'bah.

5 The Hujjaj then went to Mina in the 8th day of Thul Hijjah. Mina is a huge area outside of Makkah where people spend one night. They spend their time praying, making du'aa', reading Qur'an, and performing other kinds of worship.

6 Then they went to Arafah. It is an area where Hujjaj stay from morning until sun-set on the 9th day of the month of Thul Hijjah. They spent their time praying, making du'aa', repenting from all past sins, reading Qur'an, and engaging in other kinds of worship.

Hujjaj remember the Day of Judgment, when all people will gather in one place.

7 After sunset, Bilal and Sarah's parents left Arafah for a nearby area called Al-Muzdalifah. They prayed Maghrib and Isha, and they made du'aa' and thikr there. They slept that night in Al-Muzdalifah. In the morning, the Hujjaj returned back to Mina. Before they left, they collected pebbles (jamrat), or tiny stones, to throw at the three symbols of Shaytan at Mina. They did that over the next three or four days.

What does this act remind you of?

This part of the Hajj symbolizes the action of Prophet Ibraheem when Shaytan tried to stop him in three places on his way to sacrifice his son Isma'eel. Ibraheem threw stones at Shaytan to get him out of his way. The Hujjaj do the same. They remember that they should get Satan out of their way, and never follow his way.

8 They chose to stay three or four more days in Mina. There, they cut their hair. They also sacrificed an animal; the hujjaj sacrifice a sheep, a cow, or a camel to give to the poor and the needy. This reminds us about the ram Allah gave to Ibraheem to sacrifice in place of his son Isma'eel.

9 During these three or four days, both parents went back to Makkah again and did tawaf around Al-Ka'bah. This is called Tawaf-ul-Ifadah.

10 Then, Bilal and Sarah's parents stayed in Makkah for as long as they wanted. Before leaving Makkah, they made the farewell Tawaf (Tawaf-ul-Wadaa'). It is like saying goodbye to Al-Ka'bah, the greatest House of Allah ﷻ on Earth.

Bilal and Sarah were very happy that their mom and dad were finally home. Their parents told them all the good things about Hajj. "May Allah accept your Hajj," the children said. They were glad that their parents had returned safely, and they loved the gifts that they had brought with them.

LIKE A NEW BORN BABY!

Did you know that when people perform Hajj, their sins are washed away? The Prophet ﷺ said that whoever goes to Hajj and does not commit bad deeds, comes back like a new born baby with all of his sins washed away.

WE HAVE LEARNED

❶ Hajj is one of the five pillars of Islam.

❷ A Hajj that is free from bad deeds washes all sins away.

❸ Hajj teaches people to be patient.

❹ Hajj helps us remember the Day of Judgment.

❺ Hajj teaches us to be kind to the poor and needy.

❻ Hajj reminds us of the blessings of Allah.

❼ Hajj brings us closer to Allah.

WORDS OF WISDOM
Hadeeth Shareef

حديث شريف

Narrated by Al-Bukhari & Muslim

عن أبي هريرة رضي الله عنه: قال رسول الله ﷺ :

"من حج هذا البيت فلم يفسق ولم يرفث رجع كيوم ولدته أمه." رواه البخاري ومسلم

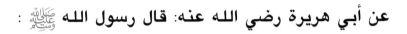

TRANSLITERATION

"Man hajja hatha lbayt falam yafsuq wa lam yarfuth raja'a kayawmi waladat-hu ammuh"

Abu Hurayra رضي الله عنه reported that Rasoolullah ﷺ said:

"Whosoever performs Hajj without making sins and mistakes, he will be coming back [pure of sins] like when he was first born."

HAJJ

We will all go to Makkah on the Hajj.

We wear only two white garments on the Hajj.

We will walk around the Ka'abah seven times.

We run backwards and run forwards on the Hajj.

We will drink the Zam-Zam water on the Hajj.

We throw pebbles at the Shaytan on the Hajj.

We will sacrifice for Allah on the Hajj.

We will all go to Makkah on the Hajj.

Listen to this nasheed on Track 6 of your CD.

ACTIVITY time

1. Watch a movie about Hajj with your friends.

2. Do a Hajj simulation: You and your friends make a Hajj in your school at the time of Hajj.

Study  Questions

1 Why is Hajj so important to Muslims?

2 Where do Muslims do Hajj?

3 Name the places the Hujjaj go to during Hajj. Describe briefly what they do there.

4 What does throwing stones at the jamrat symbolize?

5 What is the first thing the Hujjaj do in Hajj? And what is the last thing?

① What is wudoo'? Why is it important?
② How can we do wudoo' the right way?
③ What mistakes can we make when making wudoo'?

Word Watch

[Wudoo' وضوء]

﴿ يَٰٓأَيُّهَا ٱلَّذِينَ ءَامَنُوٓاْ إِذَا قُمۡتُمۡ إِلَى ٱلصَّلَوٰةِ فَٱغۡسِلُواْ وُجُوهَكُمۡ وَأَيۡدِيَكُمۡ إِلَى ٱلۡمَرَافِقِ وَٱمۡسَحُواْ بِرُءُوسِكُمۡ وَأَرۡجُلَكُمۡ إِلَى ٱلۡكَعۡبَيۡنِ ﴾

O you who believe, when you rise for Salah, (prayer) wash your faces and your hands up to the elbows, and make Mash (wiping by hands) of your heads and (wash) your feet up to the ankles... (6) Surah Al-Maeda 5: 6

Story Time

Once, Al-Hasan and Al-Husayn, the grandsons of Rasoolullah, saw an old man making wudoo'. The old man was not making wudoo' the right way. Al-Hasan and Al-Husayn wanted to teach the man how to perform wudoo' correctly. But they were not sure how to do that without hurting the man's feelings. They wanted to be very polite and respectful with him. Allah and the Prophet ordered Muslims to be respectful of those who are older. They had a great idea. What do you think they did?

Al-Hasan and Al-Husayn came to the man.
"Assalamu alaykum," they said.
"Wa Alaykum Assalam young boys," the man answered.
"Uncle, we would like you to judge which one of us makes his wudoo' better," said Al-Hasan.
"Would you, Uncle?" Al-Husayn asked.
"All right boys, if you want me to," the man answered.

Al-Hasan started making wudoo' in front of the man, and he did it very well. He started with "Bismillah" and he washed all the wudoo' parts very well. He did not speak or laugh during wudoo'. After he finished, he said the shahadah as the Prophet had taught him.

The man was impressed by Al-Hasan making wudoo'. Now it was Al-Husayn's turn; he also did his wudoo' perfectly.

"Who did his wudoo' better, Uncle?" they asked.

The man was surprised at how well they had performed their wudoo'. They had done even better than he could. He said, "MashaAllah, you both did your wudoo' very well, even better than I do. I really learned from you how a Muslim should do his wudoo' correctly."

Al-Hasan and Al-Husayn were very happy that they had taught the man to perform his wudoo' correctly, and they had done it without hurting his feelings.

"Assalamu alaykum, Uncle, and thank you for your time," they said as they left the man.

"Wa Alaykum Assalam, Good Boys," the old man answered.

healthy
habit

Always respect those who are much older than you, even when they make mistakes. You can correct them, but in a very, very polite way, just as Al-Hasan and Al-Husayn did.

Did you know that the Ummah of Prophet Muhammad ﷺ will have a shining light (Noor) in special places on their bodies on the Day of Judgment? That is how Prophet Muhammad ﷺ will know his Ummah. Where do you think this light comes from?

This light comes from wudoo'. The parts of our body that are washed by water during wudoo' will shine brightly on the Day of Judgment. That is why we should be extra careful to perform wudoo' correctly.

Wudoo' or Ablution

Wudoo,' or ablution, is the method we use to wash ourselves when we prepare for salah (prayer). Our Prophet ﷺ showed us how to make wudoo' the right way. He told us that whoever makes wudoo' the right way will have his sins forgiven by Allah.

When Do I Need Wudoo'?

Sometimes we stay pure for a long while after wudoo', but there are times when we need to renew our wudoo'.
1. When we use the bathroom
2. When we pass gas
3. If we fall asleep before salah

What Kind Of Water Do I Need?

Can we use apple juice, milk, or honey to make wudoo'? Can we use any of these things to take a bath or wash our clothing with? Of course not. We have to use pure water. Pure water ماء طهور is water that does not have a color, taste, or smell. Examples of pure water are tap water, rainwater, spring water, ice water, river water, and seawater. These are all types of pure water that are fine for wudoo'.

How Do I Make Wudoo'?

You probably learned how to make wudoo' when you were seven years old, or even younger. Sometimes, you may see your friends performing wudoo' incorrectly. It is important to remember how to make wudoo' correctly so Allah will accept your salah.

We have to make sure that water has touched every part of the body where wudoo' is made.

The steps for wudoo' are easy, but they have to be done in order, and they are as follows:

1. Niyyah- the intention for making wudoo',
2. Saying "Bismillah," which means, "in the Name of Allah." Wash the hands up to the wrists, three times. Be sure to clean between the fingers, starting with the right hand.
3. Rinse out your mouth three times. Clean your teeth with your fingers.
4. Clean the nostrils, three times, by sniffing water in and out.
5. Wash your face three times with both hands, from the top of the forehead to the bottom of the chin, and from ear to ear.
6. Wash the right arm three times up to the far end of the elbow, and above that if you can, and then do the same for the left arm.
7. Wipe your head with your wet hands once. Start from the forehead to the back of your neck, and wipe it back to the front of the head.
8. Clean inside and outside your ears once.
9. Wash the right foot up to the ankle, three times. Do the same with the left foot. Be sure to clean between your toes. It is good to wash a little above the ankles if you can.

Now your wudoo' is complete, and done according to the Sunnah!

Q. Do You know that Jannah has eight gates? Do you wish to enter Jannah from any one of them?

A. The Prophet ﷺ told us that all eight gates of Jannah will open for the person who makes a good wudoo' and says:

أشهد أن لا إله إلا الله، وأشهد أن محمدا عبده ورسوله
اللهم اجعلني من التوابين، واجعلني من المتطهرين

" Ashhadu An La Ilaha Illa Allah, Wa Ashhadu Anna Muhammadan Abduhu Wa Rasuluhu. Allahumma-j'alnee minat-tawwabin wa-j'alnee minal mutatahhireen."

" I bear witness that there is no God but Allah, and I bear witness that Muhammad is his Servant and Messenger. Oh Allah, make me among those who repent, and those who are pure."

If a person says this after wudoo', that person can enter Jannah from any gate he or she wishes. This is what Rasoolullah ﷺ said.

Wudoo'

W is for Wudoo'

We must keep our minds and bodies clean,

Because by Allah we are always seen.

Whenever you hear the call of athan,

Prepare and come pray as soon as you can.

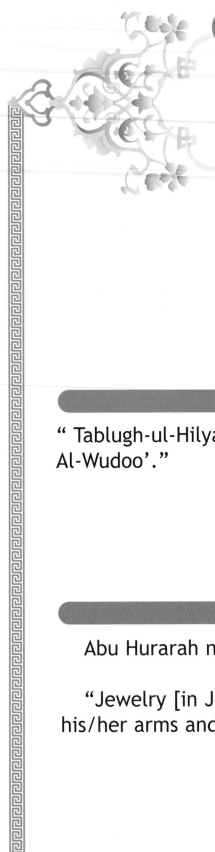

WORDS OF WISDOM
Hadeeth Shareef

حديث شريف

عن ابي هريرة رضي الله عنه قال رسول الله ﷺ :

"تبلغ الحلية من المؤمن حيث يبلغ الوضوء"

رواه مسلم

TRANSLITERATION

" Tablugh-ul-Hilyatu Mina Al-Mu'mini Haythu Yablughu Al-Wudoo'. "

MEANING TRANSLATION

Abu Hurarah narrated that The Prophet ﷺ Said:

"Jewelry [in Jannah] will cover the believer wherever (in his/her arms and legs) his wudoo' reaches."

Reported by Muslim

ACTIVITY time

Wudoo' Perfection Activity
Imagine that a Muslim company that wants to develop a video on how to make wudoo' tapes you while making wudoo'. Let your parent or a friend videotape you. Then view the tape with your parents and discover how good your wudoo' was. Write a script that identifies your mistakes.

Think Critically

Cause and Effect: What does a person lose when he or she does not perform complete wudoo'?

Study  Questions

1 What is wudoo'? What is another word that is used for it?

2 What are the steps of a complete wudoo'?

3 What kind of water can you use for wudoo'?

4 What are examples of pure water?

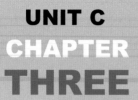
Perfect Your Prayer

Questions?

1. What is more important, to play or to pray?
2. Can we move around or play when we pray?
3. Should we perfect our prayers?
4. How can we perfect our prayer?

Word Watch

Salah	صلاة
Surah	سورة
Suwar	سُوَر
Khushoo'	خُشوع

One day, Bilal and Zaid were playing at Bilal's house. They were in the middle of a very interesting game when they heard the call to prayer coming from the Athan clock. It was time to pray 'Asr. Bilal and Zaid listened respectfully to the Athan and recited the du'aa' that comes after the Athan.

Zaid: We still have time to pray. Let's finish our game first, and then we'll pray.

Bilal: But Zaid, the most beloved deed to Allah is prayer right on time. I would rather pray first. There will be plenty of time to finish our game after we pray.

Zaid: I guess you're right, but I don't feel like leaving the game right now. I'm having so much fun!

Bilal: I'm having a lot of fun, too! But praying to Allah is more important than playing a game. I love Allah more than I love this game. I would rather meet Allah in my prayer right on time.

Zaid: Wow, Bilal, I never thought of it that way. I want to pray now, too!

Bilal and Zaid carefully made Wudoo'. Then, they laid out their prayer rugs in the direction of the Qiblah. Bilal combed his hair and tucked his shirt in nicely.

Zaid: Why are you doing that now, Bilal?

Bilal: I got a little messy while we were playing. I am about to meet Allah in my prayer, I want to look my best. I try to perfect my prayer in every way.

Zaid: Can you teach me how to perfect my prayer?

Bilal: Sure, Zaid! I start by facing the Qiblah.

Zaid: That's the direction of Al-Ka'bah in Makkah, right?

Bilal: Yes, Zaid, that's right. Then, I remind myself that I am standing in front of Allah. He is the One Who created me and the King of the entire universe. I feel very special and close to Allah when I pray. I also feel a strong love and respect for Allah in my heart. I stand very still out of respect for Allah.

Zaid: Some people move around when they are praying. They tap their foot or scratch their head a lot. Some people even look around while they are praying.

Bilal: This is wrong to do. I try not to make unnecessary movements, and I try to look down, right in front of me. This way I won't get distracted by things going on around me. Then, I make the niyyah, or the intention in my heart to pray. For example, now I will make the intention to pray Salat-ul-'Asr. Once I raise my hands up and say "Allahu Akbar," I know that I am speaking with Allah and cannot talk to anybody else.

I fold my right hand over my left hand in front of me and place them somewhere between my navel and my chest.

Then, I say Du'aa Al-Istiftah, The Supplication of Beginning the Prayer:

سُبحانَكَ اللّهُمَّ وَبِحَمْدِكَ، وتَبارَكَ اسْمُكَ، وَتَعالى جَدُّكَ، ولا إلهَ غَيْرُك

"Subhanak-Allahumma wa bi hamdika, wa tabaraka ismuka, wa ta'ala jeduka, wa la illahi ghairuka."

This means: "Glory be to You, Oh Allah, and all praise. May Your Name be blessed, and Your Might exalted. There is no god but You."

After that, I ask Allah to protect me from Shaytan by saying:

أَعُوذُ بِاللّهِ مِنَ الشَّيطانِ الرَّجيم

"A'oothu billahi mina-shaytan-ir-rajeem"

And then I recite the Fatihah and a short surah in Arabic. I try to focus on the beautiful meaning of what I am reciting. I remind myself that Allah is listening to me reciting His Qur'an.

Zaid: Do you recite the same surah in different rak'aat?

Bilal: No, I only repeat Surat-ul-Fatihah in every rak'ah; after that I recite different suwar in different rak'aat. I also make sure to recite them in the correct order.

Zaid: How long should the surah be?

Bilal: It could be as short as three ayahs or verses. However, I have been working on memorizing longer suwar that I can recite when I am praying alone.

Zaid: What do you do after you recite the Fatihah and a surah?

Bilal: I say "Allahu Akbar" and bow down by bending at the waist and placing my hands at my knees. It's an amazing feeling to bow down to Allah. I say three times:

سُبحانَ رَبيَ العظيم

"Subhana rabbiyal 'atheem."
"Glory be to my Great Lord."

Then, I say:

سَمِعَ اللهُ لِمَنْ حمِدَه

"Sami' Allahu liman hami-dah."

This means: "Allah hears those who praise Him."

And I return to a standing position with my arms at my sides. At this point, I say:

رَبَّنا لكَ الْحَمْد

"Rabbana lakal hamd."

"Oh Lord, to You belongs all praise."

Then, I say "Allahu Akbar" and kneel down on the floor to make sujood. I carefully place my hands on the ground on either side of my head and keep my elbows up. I make sure that my hands, knees, and toes are on the ground. I also make sure that my nose and forehead are touching the ground.

I say three times: سُبحانَ رَبِيَ الأعْلى

"Subhana rabbiyal a'la."

"Glory be to my Lord Most High."

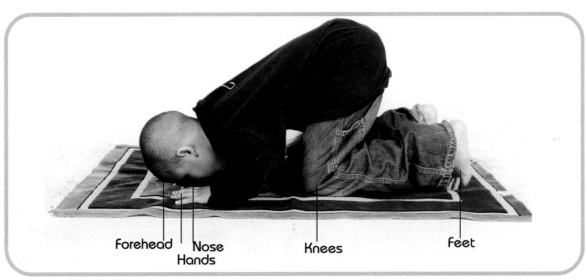

Forehead   Nose   Knees   Feet
            Hands

When I am kneeling down to Allah like this I feel very humble. I feel that I am very low, and He is very high. I remind myself that I am Allah's slave, and He is my Great Master. I am closest to Allah when I am in sujood. I feel a strong love for Him, and at the same time I feel His love for me.

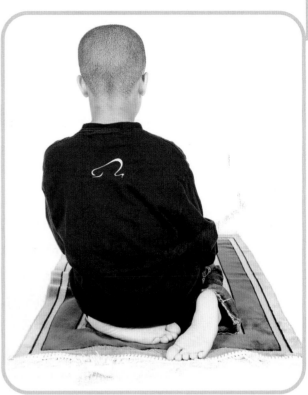

I then say "Allahu Akbar" and sit up on my knees for a moment. I can say du'aa' during this time.

I say "Allahu Akbar" and make sujood again.

Zaid: During the second sujood you say the same thing three times again.

Bilal: That's right, Zaid. Then, I say "Allahu Akbar" and stand up for the second rak'ah. This completes one rak'ah. During the second rak'ah, I repeat everything starting with the Fatihah.

Zaid: At the end of the second rak'ah you remain seated, right?

Bilal: Right! When I sit up from sujood, I remain seated and say At-Tashahhud.

At-Tashahhud

التَّحِيَّاتُ لِلّهِ والصَّلواتُ والطَّيِّبَاتِ ، السَّلامُ عليكَ أَيُّها النَّبِيُّ وَرَحْمَةُ اللهِ وبَرَكاتُه، السَّلامُ علينا وعَلَى عِبادِ اللهِ الصَّالِحِين ، أَشْهَدُ أَنْ لا إِلهَ إلااللهُ وأَشْهَدُ أَنَّ مُحَمَّداً عَبْدُهُ وَرَسولُهُ

At-Tahiyat lillah, Wassalawatu wattayyibat, As-Salamu Alayka Ayuhan-nabiyyu Wa Rahmatullahi wa barakatuh, As-Salamu Alayna Wa 'Ala 'ibadullah-is-saliheen. Ash-hadu Anna La Illaha Illallah, Wa Ash-hadu Anna Muhammadan Abduhu wa Rasooluh."

This means: "Greetings to Allah, and all prayers and purities. Peace be upon you, Oh Prophet, and Allah's Mercy and Blessings. Peace be upon us and all of Allah's righteous servants. I bear witness that there is no god but Allah and Muhammad is His servant and Messenger."

When I say this, I feel I am speaking directly with Allah. I also feel I am sending greetings directly to the Prophet. When I bear witness that there is no god but Allah, I raise my right index finger and remember that Allah is One.

If I want to pray more rak'aat, I say "Allahu Akbar," stand up, and repeat everything starting with the

Fatihah. If I want to end my prayer, I recite As-Salat ul-Ibraheemiyyah. It goes like this:

As-Salat ul-Ibraheemiyyah

اللهمَّ صلِّ على مُحَمَّدٍ وعَلى آلِ محمَّدٍكما صَلَّيْتَ على إبراهيمَ وعلى آلِ إبراهيم، وبارِكْ على مُحَمَّدٍ وعَلى آلِ محمَّدٍ كما بارَكْتَ على إبراهيمَ وعلى آلِ إبراهيم، في العالَمينَ إنّك حَميدٌ مَجيد

Allahumma salli ala Muhammadin wa ala aali Muhammad, kama sallayta ala Ibraheema wa ala aali Ibraheem, wa barik ala Muhammadin wa ala aali Muhammad, kama barakta ala Ibraheema wa ala aal Ibraheem, fil aalameena innaka Hameedun Majeed.

"Oh Allah, send our prayers upon Prophet Muhammad and the people of Prophet Muhammad as You have sent your prayers upon Prophet Ibraheem and the people of Prophet Ibrahim, and send your blessings upon Prophet Muhammad and the people of Prophet Muhammad as You have sent your blessings upon Prophet Ibraheem and the people of Prophet Ibraheem. You are worthy of all praise."

(islamcan.com/salat/duas/index.shtml)

At this point, I can say a du'aa' to Allah.

Then, I turn my face to the right and say:

السَّلامُ عَليكمْ وَرَحمَةُ اللهِ وَبَرَكاتُه

"Assalamu Alaikum warahmatullah."

And I turn my face to the left and say:

السَّلامُ عَليكمْ وَرَحمَةُ اللهِ وَبَرَكاتُه

"Assalamu Alaikum warah-matullah,"
"Peace and blessings be upon you."

When I do this I am greeting everyone who is praying with me. When I am praying alone, I remind myself that the angels are praying with me, and that there are angels on my right and on my left all the time. This part of the prayer is called tasleem.

Zaid: That is very beautiful! Let's pray now. I would like to pray as perfectly as I can.

Khushoo' During the Prayer

Bilal and Zaid prayed Salat ul-'Asr together. They went through every step carefully and respectfully. When they were finished, Bilal looked at Zaid and saw that he was crying!

Bilal: Oh Zaid, why are you crying?!
Zaid: I'm not sure. I think I am crying because I love Allah so much! While I was praying, I did everything you taught me, and I reminded myself that Allah was watching me, and that I was speaking with Him. It felt amazing.

Bilal: Masha Allah, Zaid. This is called khushoo'. Khushoo' means that you feel humble when you stand in front of Allah. It means that you focus on your prayer and that you are not distracted by other things. Khushoo' means that you feel a strong love for Allah in your heart while you pray. Some people have so much khushoo' when they pray that it makes them cry. This is what you felt.

Zaid: Allah is so great, and I am not always as good as I should be. From now on, I will always try to pray right on time, and I will always try to perfect my prayer insha Allah.

Bilal: Me too, insha Allah!

WORDS OF WISDOM
Hadeeth Shareef

حديث شريف

Narrated By Muslim, Tirmidhi & Ibn Maja

عن أَبِي مالك الأشعري رضي الله عنه: قال رسول الله ﷺ:
"الصلاة نور"

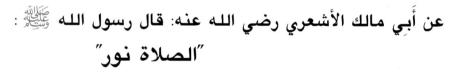

"Assalatu Noor"

MEANING TRANSLATION

Abu Malik al-Ash'ari, may Allah be pleased with him, relates that the Messenger of Allah, peace and blessings be upon him, said, "Prayer is light." (Reported by Muslim, Tirmithi and Ibn Majah)

Praying Always and on Time

When asked about the best of works, the Prophet, peace and blessings be upon him, replied, "Prayer at its time" (Bukhari 527, Muslim 85).

Once a young companion of the Prophet named Rabi'ah bin Ka'ab came to the Prophet. Rabi'ah was 14 years old. He wanted to be with the Prophet in Jannah. The Prophet asked him, "Is there anything else that you want, Rabi'ah?" Rabi'ah answered, "No, all that I want is to be with you in Jannah." The Prophet said:

أَعِنّي عَلى نَفسِكَ بِكَثْرَةِ السُّجود

"Then, help yourself by making plenty of salah."

Make sure that you pray all of your salah and sunnah salah on time, and you will be with the Prophet in Jannah, too, insha Allah!

ACTIVITY time

Divide into groups and appoint one person from each group to present two Rak'aat of prayer to the class. Go over every step together and prepare this person to make the best prayer. Then, all of the students who are appointed to present the prayer should step outside of the classroom. Your teacher will call them in one by one to present the prayer. As each student presents the prayer, the class should count and write down any mistakes. The class will then judge who presented the best prayer, and which group won.

Think Critically

Prophet Muhammad taught us that we are the closest to Allah when we are in sujood. Why do think this is so?

If a person prays by doing and saying everything perfectly, but his mind is distracted from the prayer and his heart is not with Allah, is his prayer perfect? Why or why not?

Study  Questions

1. What do you do in your heart right before you start the prayer?
2. What do you do to start the prayer?
3. How many rukoo' and sujood are there in one rak'ah of prayer?
4. What do you say in rukoo'? What do you say in sujood?
5. What do you do when you are reciting the Tashahhud?
6. What are the positions of salah called?
7. What is a good thing to do right after you finish praying?
8. What is khushoo'?

Salat-ul-Jama'ah: A Prayer Allah loves

① What is the importance of Salat-ul-Jama'ah?
② How do you pray in Jama'ah?
③ Where do we pray Salat ul-Jama'ah?

Main Idea: Salat ul-Jama'ah in the masjid is important for the individual and the Muslim community.

Word **Watch**

Salat ul-Jama'ah	صلاةُ الجماعة
Qiyam ul-Layl	قيامُ الليل
Imam	إمــام
Ma'moom	مأمــوم
Ma'moomah	مأمومة

People to Learn About:

Abdullah Ibn Umm Maktoom رضي الله عنها
Abdullah Ibn Abbas رضي الله عنه
Maymoonah رضي الله عنها

Why do you think Allah ordered Muslims to build masajid? Is it only to pray Salat ul-Jumu'ah, or Friday prayer, once a week? Or only to pray Taraweeh during Ramadan? Of course not. Allah wants us to visit the masjid every day. After all, the masjid is the house of Allah.

Once a blind man came to Rasoolullah ﷺ and said: "O Rasoolullah, I am a blind man, and my house is a little far from the masjid. Could I get permission not to come to the masjid every day?"

The prophet ﷺ first said "Yes." The man left, then Rasoolullah ﷺ quickly called him back and asked him:

"Do you hear athan, the call to prayer?"

"Yes," the man replied. Then Rasoolullah ﷺ said:

"Then you should answer the call." This means that it is better to come to the masjid for the daily prayers.

Although the man was blind, Rasoolullah wanted him to come to the masjid every day. Why? Because by doing that he earned a lot of reward and blessings. He also learned much more about Islam than if he prayed at home.

Later, Abdullah Ibn Ummi Maktoom, the blind man, became a great Muslim. The Prophet ﷺ trusted him and made him a mu'athin. He made the athan in the masjid. Also, Abdullah was sometimes chosen as a leader of Madinah when the Prophet ﷺ was traveling outside the city.

The Prophet ﷺ used to check whether his sahabah came to Salat ul-Jama'ah or not. He became upset with those who were often absent without good reasons. He understood when they were absent because they were sick or traveling outside of Madinah.

WORDS OF WISDOM
Hadeeth Shareef

حديث شريف

Narrated By Bukhari, Muslim & Tirmithi

عن عبداللـه ابن عمر رضي اللـه عنه: قال رسول اللـه ﷺ :
"صلاة الجماعة أفضل من صلاة الرجل وحده بسبع وعشرين درجة."

TRANSLITERATION

Ibn Abdullah Ibn Omar رضي الله عنه reported that the Prophet ﷺ said: "Salat-ul-Jama'ah afdal min salat-ir-rajal wahdahu bis-ab'in wa'ishreena darajah."

MEANING TRANSLATION

Rasoolullah ﷺ said, " Salah in jama'ah (together) is twenty-seven times better than praying alone."(This means that: Allah gives twenty-seven times more reward than when praying alone.)

Abdullah Ibn Abbas prays Jama'ah with the Prophet

Once, when Abdullah Ibn Abbas was a young boy, he went to spend the night at his aunt Maymoonah's house. His aunt was the wife of Prophet Muhammad. Rasoolullah ﷺ made wudoo', prayed four rak'aat, then he went to sleep. Later on, a little before Fajr time, Rasoolullah ﷺ woke up again to pray extra prayers for the sake of Allah ﷾ . This is called "Qiyam ul-layl."

Abdullah watched Rasoolullah praying. He always loved to be close to the Prophet. He wanted a big reward from Allah, too. So Abdullah joined the Prophet and prayed Jama'ah with him.

Shaytan, of course, did not like Abdullah's idea. In fact, Shaytan was very upset to see Abdullah get up, make wudoo', and stand next to Rasoolullah ﷺ to pray Salat ul-jama'ah.

Shaytan became very angry because Abdullah was earning twenty seven times more reward by praying jama'ah than he would have had if he had prayed alone.

When **Abdullah Ibn Abbas** رضي الله عنه joined the Prophet ﷺ in prayer, he made a little mistake. Instead of standing on the right side of Rasoolullah ﷺ, Abdullah stood on his left side. The Prophet ﷺ moved Abdullah to his right side, and they both prayed thirteen rak'aat for the sake of Allah ﷻ.

Abdullah felt very happy. He enjoyed being the **Ma'moom** (follower) while Rasoolullah ﷺ was the **Imam** (the prayer leader).

He learned that one must stand to the right of the imam if there are only two people doing Salat ul-Jama'ah.

If a woman is the Ma'moom, she needs to stand behind the Imam.

Rasoolullah ﷺ made a du'aa' to Allah to make Abdullah a wise scholar of Islam.

Allah responded to the Prophet's du'aa', and **Abdullah Ibn Abbas** became one of the greatest scholars of Islam.

Check Your Understanding

❶ What is the name of the young boy who went to sleep at Maymoonah's house?

❷ Who is Maymoonah?

❸ What did Rasoolullah ﷺ do before Fajr time ?

❹ What did Abdullah decide to do when he saw Rasoolullah praying?

❺ Where do people stand when the Ma'moom is:
One male?
One female?
More than one follower?

Think Critically

How can Salat ul-Jama'ah make our Muslim society strong?

Study  Questions

1 What do we call this kind of salah?

Questions?

1. Have you been to the masjid before?
2. Did you see how Muslims pray in a group?
3. How is Salat ul-Jama'ah different from praying alone?
4. What do we call the one who leads in Salat ul-Jama'ah?
5. Can women and girls pray in Jama'ah?

Main Idea: Read to find out how to pray Salat ul-Jama'ah in the masjid, at home, or in school. Please read carefully. This chapter is challenging!

Word Watch

| Salat ul-Jama'ah | صلاة الجماعة |
| Salat ul-Masbooq | صلاة المسبوق |

Praying Salatul-Jama'ah

Where do we Pray Salat ul-Jama'ah?

Usually **Salat ul-Jama'ah** is done in the masjid. The Prophet ﷺ and the Sahabah used to pray almost every salah in the masjid. However, a Muslim can pray Jama'ah in school, at work, or at home, if he has a good reason for not being able to go to the masjid.

When do we pray Jama'ah?

Muslims pray Jama'ah in the masjid shortly after the prayer time begins and the Athan is called. Muslims pray Salat ul-Jama'ah in the masjid five times a day.

Who should pray Salat ul-Jama'ah?

Allah and the Prophet encouraged all Muslims to pray Salat ul-Jama'ah in the masjid whenever they can. However, women are excused from praying in the masjid, especially if they are busy at home. Praying in the masjid can be hard on mothers and wives, especially if they have small children.

Praying Salat ul-Jama'ah

1. Where should I stand?

Usually, the imam stands in the front and middle. The men line up behind the imam, and boys line up behind the men. Girls line up behind the boys, and the women are behind them.

So this is what you should do:
Stand in line and make sure your **line is straight**.

Ma'moom   Imam

If there is a **male imam** and **one male Ma'moom**, the ma'-moom stands on the right side of the imam. The same thing if there is a female imam and female ma'moomah.

Imam

Ma'moomah

If there is a **male imam** and **one female ma'moomah**, the female ma'moomah stands behind the imam.

2. How Should I Follow the Imam?

■ Follow the imam in every move that he makes during the prayer.

■ When the imam says Allahu akbar out loud, you should say it quietly to yourself.

■ When the imam reads the Qur'an loudly, you listen to him. Only read Al-Fatihah and other surahs when the imam is silent.

■ Make the movements of salah after the imam does them. Just wait a second or two after he has made a move, then follow it. For example, after the imam makes rukoo,' you make rukoo'. Also, after he makes sujood, you make sujood. You do not move with him or before him, you only move after him.

■ Do not make unnecessary moves, like looking around, scratching your head, or bumping into the people around you. Be calm and concentrate 100% on the prayer.

Do you do that already?

Takbeer!
Give yourself a pat on the back.
Masha'Allah you are very well disciplined in salah!

Salat-ul-Masbooq: What do you do if you miss some rak'aat?

If you came to the masjid late and find that you have missed one or more rak'ah, do NOT worry, and don't run. Just walk calmly in and join the Jama'ah. Join the last line of prayer, so you do not disturb those in front of you, and follow the imam.

When the imam makes tasleem, do not make tasleem. Stand up and pray the rak'aat you missed. You count the rak'aat you prayed with the imam to determine how many rak'aat you missed.

For example,

If you **pray 3 rak'aat** of the asr prayer with the imam, then you know that you missed 1 rak'ah. After the imam finishes his tashahhud and tasleem, you cannot make tasleem. You have to get up and make the final rak'ah as you normally would, then say your tashahhud and then your tasleem.

If you **pray two rak'aat** of the Asr prayer with the imam, then you know that you missed two rak'ahs. After the imam finishes his tashahhud and tasleem, you don't make tasleem; get up and make up the remaining two rak'aat as you normally would, then say your tashahhud and your tasleem.

If you **prayed one rak'ah** of the Asr prayer with the jama'ah, then you know that you missed three rak'aat. Therefore you have to make up these three rak'aat on your own. So, you pray one rak'ah, and then make the first juloos, and read the first tashahhud. Then you stand and pray the two rak'aat left. Then make second juloos, read the final tashahhud, and make tasleem.

If you came in during the final sujood or tashahhud, then you did not pray any rak'ah with the jama'ah. So, you stand up and pray the full four rak'aat of Asr prayer as you normally would do it alone.

If I enter the Salat ul-jamaah in the middle of a rak'ah, how do I know if that rak'ah counts?

If you enter the salah while the imam is in qiyam or even in rukoo', then that rak'ah counts. If you join after the rukoo', like in sujood, or during tashahhud, then you've missed the rak'ah, and you need to make it up.

ACTIVITY time

Role play how to perform Sulat ul-Jama'ah if the ma'moon was:

1. One male.
2. One female.
3. Group of males and females.

Study  Questions

1. What do you do when you miss one rak'ah in the masjid?

2. What do you do when you miss two raka'at of Salat ul-Asr in the masjid?

3. What do you do when you miss three raka'at of Salat ul-Thuhr in the masjid?

4. What do you do if you came late to the masjid for Salat ul-Maghrib and found the imam sitting for the last tashahhud?

Thikr: Easy Ibadah, Great Rewards

Questions?

1. If you love someone, how often do you remember him or her, or mention his or her name?
2. How do you feel when you remember someone you love and respect?
3. How often do you remember Allah and praise Him every day?

Main Idea: Thikr is a very important type of ibadah that a Muslim should always do. It involves remembering Allah with the heart and tongue. It is an easy ibadah to do, but it has great rewards for those who practice it.

Word Watch

Thikr	ذِكْر
Tasbeeh	تسبيح
Subhan-Allah	سُبحان الله
Alhamdulillah	الحَمْدُ للّه
La ilaha illaallah	لا إله إلا الله
Allahu Akbar	الله أكبر
Subhan Allah wa bihamdihi	سُبحان الله وبحمده
Subhan Allah Al Atheem	سُبحان الله العظيم
Astaghfirullah	أستغفرُ الله
Salla Allahu Alayhi wa Sallam	صلى الله عليه وسَلَّم
A'oothu Billahi Min	أعوذ باللّه من
Ashaytan-irrajeem	الشيطان الرجيم

C48

Zaid knocked on his parents' bedroom door.

Father: Who is it?
Zaid: It is me, Dad. Zaid.
Father: Come on in, Zaid.

Zaid opened the door, slowly and politely.

Zaid: Assalamu alaykum, Father.
Father: Wa alaykum assalam, Zaid. Subhan Allah...Subhan Allah...
Zaid: What are you doing, Dad?
Father: I am doing my daily thikr.
Zaid: What is that?
Father: Thikr means remembering Allah and saying His Name.
Zaid: Why are you doing that?
Father: Because Allah encouraged us to do thikr as much as we can.

Allah says:

﴿يا أيها الذين آمنوا اذكروا الله ذِكرا كثيرا، وسبحوه بكرة وأصيلا﴾
سورة الأحزاب ٤١-٤٢

O you who believe, remember Allah abundantly, (41) And proclaim His purity at morn and eve. (42) Surah Al-Ahzab 33:41-42

Zaid: What do we get if we do thikr?
Father: Let me ask you this: What will happen to you when you eat after being hungry?
Zaid: I feel fulfilled and happy!
Father: Exactly! Thikr is a food for your soul. The food that we eat fills our body and makes it strong. The thikr that we do fills our soul and makes it strong. Allah makes us feel happy when we keep praising Allah and remembering Him. We also get great rewards and hasanat. For example, If we say subhanAllah once, we will be rewarded ten hasanat.
Zaid: Wow! Allah is so generous.
Father: Let me see if you are good in math. How many hasanat do we get if we say it one hundred times?
Zaid: One hundred times ten is one thousand. Oh! That is a lot!
Father: Great, Zaid. You can get one thousand hasanat in less than two minutes. You see, thikr is easy ibadah, but it has great rewards.
Zaid: Cool! I will do thikr all the time, just like you, Dad.
Father: Excellent, My Boy. May Allah bless you.
Zaid: Oh, Dad, I almost forgot what I came for. Can you please give me a dollar? I want to buy something from the store.
Father: [Laughing] Okay, Son. Here is a dollar.

1. The Trees of Jannah:

سبحان الله والحمدُ لله ولا إله إلا الله
والله أكبر

Subhan Allah walhamdulillah wa la ilaha illallah Wallahu Akbar

Subhan Allah walhamdulillah wa la ilaha illallah Wallahu Akbar

The Prophet ﷺ said:

"Allah loves these words the most. And they are the best words after the Qur'an. He also said that if we say it once, Allah will plant for us a tree in Jannah."

This is a great kind of thikr, because it includes four statements of thikr altogether. It includes **Tasbeeh**, Al-Hamd, Tahleel and Takbeer. As you learned earlier, we say these after the fard salah every day.

healthy habit

Say it one hundred times every day. It takes only five minutes to say, but you will gain great rewards, and a forest in Jannah.

- Tasbeeh تسبيح :

When we look at this glorious nature surrounding us, we remember it is all made by Allah ﷻ. We should say سبحان الله, Subhan Allah. This means "Glory be to Allah." It is also called Tasbeeh. For example, when I look at the beautiful blue sky, I say "Subhan Allah." When I look at the huge, high mountains, I say "Subhan Allah." When I see the moon and the stars, I say "Subhan Allah."

THE GREATEST TASBEEH:

سبحان الله وبحمده سبحان الله العظيم

Subhan Allah wa bihamdihi. Subhan Allah Al-Atheem.

The Prophet ﷺ said: "There are two words that are easy for the tongue [to say], but they are heavy on the scale [of Allah's reward], and Allah loves them:

"Subhan Allah wa bihamdihi Subhan Allah Al Atheem"

- Al-Hamd الحمد :
We also say

الحمدُ لله

Al-hamdulillah
which means: "Praise and thanks be to Allah." It is also called Al-Hamd. We say that to thank Him for all the gifts He gave us in this life: Gifts like our body and senses, the food we eat, the car we use, and the house we live in. The best gift of all is Islam.

- Tahleel تهليل :

The Best of Thikr:

لا إله إلا الله

La ilaha illallah

It means, "there is no God but Allah." This is called tahleel, which means raising the voice when mentioning Allah. The Prophet ﷺ said:

أفضل الذكر لا إله إلا الله

"The best of thikr is saying la ilaha illallah."

He also said : "The one who says every day:

لا إله إلا الله وحده لا شريك له،

له الملك وله الحمد،

وهو على كل شيئ قدير

"There is no god but Allah alone, who has no partner, His is the kingdom [of the universe], and to Him belongs the high praise. And He is capable of doing everything."
He will be rewarded as if he set ten slaves free for the sake of Allah."

: تكبير - **Takbeer**

Saying

الله أكبر

Allah Akbar

is a great kind of thikr. It is called takbeer. It means "Allah is the Greatest," greater than the world, greater than all people, and greater than everything in the universe.

We say it when we make athan. We start the prayer with it, and we say it in Salat ul-Eid. We also say it when we are happy, or when we face challenges.

2. Astaghfirullah استغفر الله :

It means, "O Allah, forgive me." It is called istighfar or seeking forgiveness. Sometimes we do things that are not right that we don't mean. When this happens, Allah told us to ask for forgiveness.

We know that Allah has 99 names. One of His names is "Al-Ghafoor" (The Forgiving).

RASOOLULLAH USED TO SAY ISTIGHFAR 100 HUNDRED TIMES A DAY.

Example:

If I said a bad word that I did not mean to say, I should say, "Astaghfirullah."

أستغفر الله

أستغفر الله

I missed Asr prayer, Astaghfirullah-Al-Atheem-allathi la ilaha illa how-Al-Hayy-Al-Qayyouma wa 'atoubi ilayh

استغفر الله العظيم الذي لا إله إلا هو الحي القيوم وأتوب إليه

This is the long statement of Istighfar.

healthy habit

Say Istighfar 100 times every day as Rasoolullah used to do.

حديث شريف

Narrated By

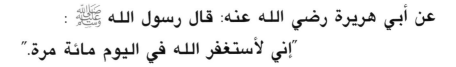

عن أبي هريرة رضي الله عنه: قال رسول الله ﷺ :
"إني لأستغفر الله في اليوم مائة مرة."

TRANSLITERATION

"Inni la-'astighfir-ullaha fil yawmi mi'ata marrah"

TRANSLATION

Abu Hurayrah رضي الله عنه reported that Rasoolullah ﷺ said:
"I ask Allah to forgive me every day one hundred times."

3. **Salla Allahu Alayhi wa Sallam:**

صلى الله عليه وسلم

It means, "Peace and bless-ings upon him." We use this term every time we say or hear the name of Prophet Muhammad ﷺ , or any other prophet.

WHAT A DEAL?

Would you like Allah ﷻ to grant you His Mercy?

Allah ﷻ will grant you ten times His Mercy if you say: " صلى الله عليه وسلم " once.

healthy
h a b i t

Say it whenever you hear the name of Rasoolullah. Also say it ten times in the morning and ten times in the evening as Rasoolullah asked us to do.

4. A'oothu Billahi Min Ashaytan-irrajeem

أعوذ بالله من الشيطان الرجيم

It means, "I seek protection with Allah from the cursed Devil." We use this term in many ways:

1) Before we start reciting Qur'an.
2) When we feel angry.
3) When Shaytan whispers to us to do something wrong, if we say " أعوذ بالله من الشيطان الرجيم " "A'oothu Billahi Min-Ashaytan Arrajeem," Shaytan becomes small and weak.

healthy

h a b i t

Say it many times every day, especially when you think of doing something wrong.

DID YOU KNOW...?

Shaytan ties three knots behind each one's head before sleeping, so we won't worship Allah ﷻ. Do you want to untie these knots? Prophet Muhammad ﷺ told us how to untie them:

1. When you get up, mention Allah's name.
2. Make wudoo'.
3. Pray Fajr.

Then you will be strong and free of Shaytan.

healthy
habit

When you make thikr, don't only say it with your tongue, but also feel it in your heart.

THIKR

Subhanallah.
We praise Allah.

Alhamdulilah.
We thank Allah.

Wa la ilaha ilallah
There is no god but Allah.
Allah is One.

Allahu Akbar.
Allah is Great.

Listen to this nasheed on Track 9 of your CD.

ACTIVITY time

PAIR UP:
In a basket, write all the terms that you have learned in this lesson on a piece of paper, and put them in the basket. Divide the classroom into groups. Let each group pick one piece of paper and act out the term written in it.

Think Critically

Why is it important to not only make Thikr with our tongues, but also with our hearts?

Study  Questions

1 What does thikr mean?

2 Say five statements of thikr?

3 What are Tasbeeh, Al-Hamd, Tahleel, Takbeer and Isti'athah?

4 What is the best type of Tasbeeh?

5 What should we say when we hear the name of Rasoolullah?

6 What is the statement of thikr that is rewarded with a tree in Jannah?

Zakah: The Third Pillar of Islam

1. What do you do with your money?
2. Do you give money to the poor?
3. How does a poor hungry child feel when he or she gets money or food?
4. What will happen to you when you give money to needy people?
5. What is the third pillar of Islam?

Main Idea: Zakah is the third pillar of Islam, and it blesses our money.

Word
Watch

Zakah	زكـاة
Sadaqah	صـدقة
Fard	فـرض

 ﴿ وَءَاتُوا۟ ٱلزَّكَوٰةَ ﴾

... pay Zakah...(78)
Surah Al-Hajj 22: 78

Zakah is the third pillar of Islam.
Giving Zakah is **fard**; this means it is required of Muslims.

What does Zakah mean?

Zakah is a donation of a small part of our savings at the end of each year. Allah commanded us to give to the needy and poor at least 2.5% of our savings every year. That is one dollar out of every 40 dollars. Allah mentioned zakah many times in the Qur'an. This shows us the importance of sharing our money with those who need it.

Did you know?

IT PURIFIES ME!

When we give Zakah, it purifies our hearts from greed and selfishness.

Story Time

Once Zaid went with his father to the bank. Zaid's father took some money from his account and told his son, "We are going to give this money for zakah."

"What is zakah?" Zaid asked.

"It is the money that Muslims must give to their needy brothers and sisters," answered his father. He continued, "Allah blesses our money and family when we give zakah. Allah has promised us that the more we give and share, the more we will receive."

"Does that mean that Allah will put more money in our bank account?" Zaid asked.

"Not exactly that way," answered his father. "Allah blesses our wealth, helps us use it in the best way, and also prevents us from wasting it."

"This tells us," Zaid's dad explained, "that the blessings we get from giving zakah are much more valuable than the money itself. And giving zakah will never make us poor or needy. Allah will always give to us if we remember others. He will reward us with Jannah, too."

Zaid learned a lot from his trip to the bank with his father, and he said, "When I grow up, I will always pay zakah and give charity to help others."

WORDS OF WISDOM
Hadeeth Qudsi Shareef

حديث شريف

Narrated By Bukhari & Muslim

عن أبي هريرة رضي الله عنه: قال رسول الله ﷺ إن الله يقول:

"أنفق يا ابن آدم، أنفق عليك" رواه البخاري ومسلم

TRANSLITERATION

"Inna Allah yaqool: anfiq ya-bna adam, anfiq 'alayk."

MEANING TRANSLATION

Abu Hurayrah رضي الله عنه reported that the Prophet ﷺ said: "Allah says, 'O son of Adam, if you spend (on the needy), I will spend on you.'"

Sadaqah: Optional Charity

If we still have extra money after we give zakah, we can give more money to earn more hasanat, or rewards. This extra donation is called sadaqah, or charity.

Some people think sadaqah only means giving money. But we can give sadaqah in many other ways if we do not have money.

Here are some other kinds of sadaqah:

❶ Smiling at others is a sadaqah.
❷ Removing something harmful from the road is a sadaqah.
❸ Sharing our lunch with someone who forgot his is a sadaqah.
❹ Picking up litter is a sadaqah.
❺ Helping someone carry a heavy load is a sadaqah.
❻ Saying a kind word is a sadaqah.

WORDS OF WISDOM
Hadeeth Shareef

حديث شريف

Narrated By Tirmithi & Ahmad

عن أبي كبشة رضي الله عنه: قال رسول الله ﷺ :

"ما نقص مال من صدقة" رواه الترمذي وأحمد

TRANSLITERATION

"Ma naqasa malun min sadaqah"

MEANING TRANSLATION

Abu Kabsha رضي الله عنه reported that the Prophet ﷺ said: "Charity never decreases money."

Did you know when you give charity, Allah ﷻ multiplies it for you on the Day of Judgment. The more you give, the more Allah ﷻ will give you.

Story Time

MY GARDEN BELONGS TO ALLAH!

Once a person was walking through the fields. Suddenly he heard a voice in the sky: "**O clouds, go and rain over the garden of So and So.**" The voice mentioned the name of the owner of that garden. The man on the ground was surprised. He saw the clouds moving toward a garden so he followed them. A short while after, rain started to fall on that garden. The man was amazed. He looked for the garden's owner and found him. He told him what he had heard and seen a while ago.

He asked him: "What do you do in order to receive this great care from Allah?"

The owner answered, "I do not do much, really. Allah is always generous with me. But, I usually divide my income from the garden into three equal parts. One part I spend on my family, another part I spend on the garden, and the third part I give to the poor."

The man said, "This explains what I saw today. You are generous, and Allah is more generous with you."

SHARE
GIVE ZAKAH AND SADAQAH

سورة البقرة

Surah Al-Baqara 2: 261

﴿ مَثَلُ ٱلَّذِينَ يُنفِقُونَ أَمْوَٰلَهُمْ فِى سَبِيلِ ٱللَّهِ كَمَثَلِ حَبَّةٍ أَنۢبَتَتْ سَبْعَ سَنَابِلَ فِى كُلِّ سُنۢبُلَةٍ مِّا۟ئَةُ حَبَّةٍ ۗ وَٱللَّهُ يُضَٰعِفُ لِمَن يَشَآءُ ۚ وَٱللَّهُ وَٰسِعٌ عَلِيمٌ ﴿٢٦١﴾ ﴾

TRANSLITERATION

"Mathalu-llatheena yunfiqoona amwalahum fee sabeeli-llahi kamathali habbatin 'anbatat sab'a sanabila fee kulli sunbu-latim mi'atu habbah, wallahu yuda'ifu limay yasha'o wal-lahu wasi'un 'aleem"

MEANING TRANSLATION

The example of those who spend in the way of Allah is just like a grain that produced seven ears, each ear having a hundred grains, and Allah multiplies (the reward) for whom He wills. Allah is All-Embracing, All-Knowing. (261)

Zakah

Zakah, Zakah! Good Muslims give Zakah
Allah has asked us one and all to give Zakah.
Zakah, Zakah! Good Muslims give Zakah
We must be sure to help the poor
Zakah, Zakah!
Zakah, Zakah! Good Muslims give Zakah.
We fast in Ramadan, and then we give Zakah.
To give in need is a good deed.
Zakah, Zakah!
Zakah, Zakah! Good Muslims give Zakah.
When we have more than what we need, we give
Zakah.
It's only fair to give our share.
Zakah, Zakah!
Zakah, Zakah! Good Muslims give Zakah.
Allah will bless us when we give Zakah
We do our part, give from our heart.
Zakah, Zakah!

Listen to this nasheed on Track 10 of your CD.

Think Critically

Some rich people do not give zakah, while others who are not as rich give zakah regularly. Why?

healthy

Give Sadaqah or charity to the poor as much as you can.
If you do that, you:
- Help your Muslim brothers and sisters
- You help in building a strong community
- You please Allah, and He will grant you Jannah, inshAllah!

Study  Questions

1 What is zakah?

2 How important is zakah? Why?

3 When do we give zakah?

4 What is sadaqah?

5 Why does Allah want us to give out zakah and sadaqah?

UNIT D

PROPHET MUHAMMAD IN MAKKAH

The New Messenger

 **Questions?**

1. What does the word **"prophet"** mean?
2. What does the word **"messenger"** mean?
3. What are the Arabic words for prophet and messenger?
4. Name some of the prophets and messengers of Allah?
5. Who was the Last Messenger?

Main Idea: Muhammad ﷺ became the Final Messenger of Allah.

 **Word Watch**

Ghar Hira'	غار حراء
Jibreel	جبريل
Jabal-un-Noor	جبل النور
Rasoolullah	رسول الله

Bilal and Zaid were excited. Their parents were going to take them to the masjid. They were going to pray jama'ah, and listen to the weekly lessons about Prophet Muhammad ﷺ . They would also play basketball with the other children. When they arrived at the masjid, they prayed jama'ah and even did the Sunnah prayer.

Shortly after that, they went to teacher Luqman, who taught them the Seerah (life story) of the Prophet each week.

Luqman: Assalamu alaikum, young brothers.
Group: Wa alaykum us-salam wa Rahmatullahi wa Barakatuh.
Luqman: Thank you all for coming this evening. Tonight I have a great lesson planned for you, and then we can all play basketball in the gym.
Group: Great! Al-Hamdulillah! We are excited.
Luqman: I am ready to start the lesson, but remember. Whenever I mention the Prophet or his name, please say salla-Allahu alayhi wa sallam, all right?
Group: Yes. Salla-Allahu alayhi wa sallam.

healthy
habit

When you are in the masjid listening to a lesson, sit politely, listen carefully, and learn. Avoid moving around or talking to those around you.

Luqman: Good, and if you need to say something, or ask a question, raise your hand first. It is not polite to interrupt others while they are speaking.
Group: All right, insha Allah.
Luqman: One last thing. Please sit still and listen carefully. Okay, let us start.

AT THE CAVE OF HIRA'

As you all know, Prophet Muhammad ﷺ was very honest and kind. He was a great and strong man. His family and friends loved and trusted him. And he was respected by his tribe, Quraysh, in Makkah. He was kind and generous to his guests, and he always fed the poor and helped the needy.

Muhammad ﷺ liked to go to a cave called "Ghar (cave) Hira'" on top of a mountain near Makkah.   Sometimes he would spend days in that cave. Prophet Muhammad ﷺ used to think about the wonderful creations of Allah ﷻ .

READ!

One night, while Muhammad ﷺ was alone at the Cave of Hira', Angel Jibreel, the leader of the angels, appeared to him. The angel surprised Muhammad ﷺ, who thought he was alone in the cave. Jibreel took Muhammad ﷺ and embraced him tightly, saying, "Read." Muhammad answered him, "I cannot read."
Jibreel squeezed Muhammad closely again and said, "Read."
Muhammad ﷺ again replied, "I cannot read."
The third time, Jibreel embraced him and said, "Read in the Name of your Lord, who created man from a clot of blood..."

Angel Jibreel read the first five verses from Surat Al-'Alaq. These were the first five verses of the Holy Qur'an to be revealed.

Allah ﷻ sent Angel Jibreel to teach Muhammad ﷺ the Message of Islam, and to tell him that Allah had chosen him to teach Islam to all peoples. Islam was not a religion for a certain tribe or people. Islam is the final Message of Allah to all mankind.

Bilal: Teacher Luqman, what does that mean?

Luqman: It means that Allah wanted someone to teach people how to believe in Him, how to worship Him, and how to be good people. So Allah chose Prophet Muhammad to teach people all that, and to guide them to the right path. Do you understand, Bilal?

Bilal: Yes, jazak Allahu khayran.

Zaid: Why did Allah choose Prophet Muhammad, not somebody else?

Luqman: Only great people can be prophets. Prophet Muhammad ﷺ was a wise, honest, and strong man. Allah knew that Muhammad ﷺ was the best man to be chosen as the last prophet, so He chose him.
All right, let's continue. From that day on, Muhammad ﷺ became a Messenger from Allah (Rasoolullah رسول الله) to all mankind.

سورة العلق

Surah Al-Alaq 96:1-19

بِسۡمِ ٱللَّهِ ٱلرَّحۡمَٰنِ ٱلرَّحِيمِ

ٱقۡرَأۡ بِٱسۡمِ رَبِّكَ ٱلَّذِى خَلَقَ ﴿١﴾ خَلَقَ ٱلۡإِنسَٰنَ مِنۡ عَلَقٍ ﴿٢﴾ ٱقۡرَأۡ وَرَبُّكَ ٱلۡأَكۡرَمُ ﴿٣﴾ ٱلَّذِى عَلَّمَ بِٱلۡقَلَمِ ﴿٤﴾ عَلَّمَ ٱلۡإِنسَٰنَ مَا لَمۡ يَعۡلَمۡ ﴿٥﴾ كَلَّا إِنَّ ٱلۡإِنسَٰنَ لَيَطۡغَىٰ ﴿٦﴾ أَن رَّءَاهُ ٱسۡتَغۡنَىٰ ﴿٧﴾ إِنَّ إِلَىٰ رَبِّكَ ٱلرُّجۡعَىٰ ﴿٨﴾ أَرَءَيۡتَ ٱلَّذِى يَنۡهَىٰ ﴿٩﴾ عَبۡدًا إِذَا صَلَّىٰ ﴿١٠﴾ أَرَءَيۡتَ إِن كَانَ عَلَى ٱلۡهُدَىٰ ﴿١١﴾ أَوۡ أَمَرَ بِٱلتَّقۡوَىٰ ﴿١٢﴾ أَرَءَيۡتَ إِن كَذَّبَ وَتَوَلَّىٰ ﴿١٣﴾ أَلَمۡ يَعۡلَم بِأَنَّ ٱللَّهَ يَرَىٰ ﴿١٤﴾ كَلَّا لَئِن لَّمۡ يَنتَهِ لَنَسۡفَعَۢا بِٱلنَّاصِيَةِ ﴿١٥﴾ نَاصِيَةٍ كَٰذِبَةٍ خَاطِئَةٍ ﴿١٦﴾ فَلۡيَدۡعُ نَادِيَهُۥ ﴿١٧﴾ سَنَدۡعُ ٱلزَّبَانِيَةَ ﴿١٨﴾ كَلَّا لَا تُطِعۡهُ وَٱسۡجُدۡ وَٱقۡتَرِب ۩ ﴿١٩﴾

TRANSLITERATION

[1] Iqra' biismi rabbik-allathee khalaq

[2] Khalaq-al'insana min 'alaq

[3] He Who taught (the use of) the pen,

[4] Allathee allama bilqalam

[5] Allamal'insana malam ya'lam

[6] Kalla inn-al-insana layatgha

[7] Ar ra'ahu-staghna

[8] Inna ila rabbik-arruj'aa

[9] Ara'ayt allathee yanha

[10] Abdan itha salla

[11] Araayta in kana ala-lhuda

[12] Aw amara bittaqwa

[13] Ara'ayta in kaththaba watawalla

[14] Alam ya'lam bi'ann-Allaha yara

[15] Kalla la'in lam yantahi lanasfa'an binnasiyah

[16] Nasiyatin kathibatin khati'ah

[17] Falyad'u nadiyah

[18] Sanad'u-zzabaniyah

[19] Kalla la tuti'hu wasjud waqtarib

Read with the name of your Lord who created (every thing), (1) He created man from a clot of blood. (2) Read, and your Lord is the most gracious, (3) Who imparted knowledge by means of the pen. (4) He taught man what he did not know. (5) In fact, man crosses the limits, (6) Because he deems himself to be free of need. (7) Surely to your Lord is the return. (8) Have you seen him who forbids (9) A servant of Allah when he prays? (10) Tell me, if he is on the right path, (11) Or bids piety, (would the former still forbid him?) (12) Tell me, if he rejects (the true faith) and turns away, (13) Does he not know that Allah is watching (him)? (14) No! If he does not desist, We will certainly drag (him) by forelock, (15) A lying, sinful forelock. (16) So let him call the men of his council, (17) We will call the soldiers of the Hell. (18) No! Never obey him, and bow down in sajdah, and come close to Me. (19)

Listen to this nasheed/Sura on Track 12 of your CD.

COVER ME! COVER ME!!!
WRAP ME UP! WRAP ME UP!!!

Luqman: How do you think Prophet Muhammad ﷺ felt?

Ahmad: I think he must have been scared. If I were in his place, I would have been so scared!

Luqman: Yes, the Prophet ﷺ was frightened. That had never happened to him before. So he decided to go back home.

When Prophet Muhammad ﷺ was leaving the cave, he heard a voice calling him. It was Angel Jibreel again. When the Prophet looked up, he saw the huge figure of Angel Jibreel, with, 600 wings filling the sky.

Group: Wow! Six hundred wings! That's a lot.

Luqman: Yes, angels are great. And Jibreel is the greatest of them all.

Zaid: Teacher Luqman, what happened next?

Luqman: Muhammad ﷺ went running home. When he arrived he was tired and anxious. He told his wife Khadeejah to cover him with a blanket. Later, he told her what had happened to him up in the cave. Khadeejah رضي الله عنه comforted Muhammad ﷺ. She told him, "Do not worry. You are honest and truthful. You help the needy and honor your guests. Allah will not abandon you. He will take good care of you."

Then Allah ﷻ sent Angel Jibreel again to Prophet Muhammad ﷺ. He ordered him to start calling on people to believe in Allah and worship Him alone. He revealed to him the first ayat of Surat Al-Muddathir.

WORDS OF WISDOM
Holy Qur'an

سورة المدثر

Surah Al-Muddaththir 74: 1-10

بِسۡمِ ٱللَّهِ ٱلرَّحۡمَٰنِ ٱلرَّحِيمِ

يَٰٓأَيُّهَا ٱلۡمُدَّثِّرُ ﴿١﴾ قُمۡ فَأَنذِرۡ ﴿٢﴾ وَرَبَّكَ فَكَبِّرۡ ﴿٣﴾ وَثِيَابَكَ فَطَهِّرۡ ﴿٤﴾ وَٱلرُّجۡزَ فَٱهۡجُرۡ ﴿٥﴾ وَلَا تَمۡنُن تَسۡتَكۡثِرُ ﴿٦﴾ وَلِرَبِّكَ فَٱصۡبِرۡ ﴿٧﴾ فَإِذَا نُقِرَ فِي ٱلنَّاقُورِ ﴿٨﴾ فَذَٰلِكَ يَوۡمَئِذٖ يَوۡمٌ عَسِيرٌ ﴿٩﴾ عَلَى ٱلۡكَٰفِرِينَ غَيۡرُ يَسِيرٍ ﴿١٠﴾

TRANSLITERATION

[1] Ya 'ayyuhal-muddaththir
[2] Qum fa'anthir
[3] Warabbaka fakabbir
[4] Wthiyabaka fatahhir
[5] War-rujza fahjur
[6} Wala tamnun tastakthir
[7] Walirabbika fasbir
[8] Fa'itha nuqira fin-naqoor
[9] Fathalika yawma 'ithiy yawmun aseer
[10] 'alal kafireena ghayru yaseer

O you, enveloped in a mantle, (1) Stand up and warn, (2) And pronounce the greatness of your Lord, (3) And purify your clothes, (4) And keep away from filth, (5) And do not do a favour (to anyone merely) to seek more (in return). (6) And for the sake of your Lord, observe patience. (7) For when the trumpet will be blown, (8)That day will be a difficult day, (9) Not easy for the disbelievers. (10)

Allah (is) An-Noor

النور

THE Light

"الله نور السموات والأرض"

Allah is the Light for the Heavens and Earth. He guides His prophets and servants to the truth. Al-Qur'an is the light of Allah on Earth.

WARAQAH THE WISE MAN

After Muhammad ﷺ calmed down, Khadeejah رضي الله عنها took him to see her cousin Waraqah Ibn Nawfal. He was a very wise man. He had vast knowledge about religions. They told Waraqah what had happened to Muhammad ﷺ at Ghar Hira'. Waraqah understood. He said: "What you saw at the mountain was an angel. Allah ﷾ sent him to all the prophets before you. Muhammad, I think you have been chosen to be the new Messenger of Allah."

Prophet Muhammad ﷺ and Khadeejah returned home. Prophet Muhammad was thinking about what he had seen on the mountain. Waraqah also made him think that he was a man with a great mission.

Khadeejah said to Muhammad, "Get some sleep and rest, Muhammad."

Prophet Muhammad replied, "The time for sleep has gone, Khadeejah." Prophet Muhammad ﷺ meant that from now on, he would not get much rest because he had a big job to do.

He became Rasoolullah, a messenger of Allah. Allah wanted him to teach all people to worship God alone and follow his true religion, **Islam**.

READ

"Read!" said the angel to Muhammad.
"Read in the name of Allah."
Allah had chosen him, Muhammad, as the Prophet of Allah.

In the cave, one dark and lonely night,
Muhammad sat alone.
He prayed that all would see the light
And worship God alone.
And in the darkness, suddenly,
He felt himself wrapped tight.
No human there that he could see, a voice spoke with great might.

"I'm not a reader," stammered he.
He felt his ribs would break.
He wondered, "Was he dreaming now,
Or was he wide awake?"
The angel squeezed three times in all,
Commanding him to read.
And finally, Muhammad asked, "What do I read?"

Muhammad quickly left the cave.
And ran across the plain.

As home he dashed, to his surprise,
The angel came again
From Earth to sky the angel stood.
The figure filled his view.
"I am Jibreel, sent from Allah, and here's what you must do"

Straight home to wise Khadeejah then
Muhammad ran in fear.
As home he ran, his tale to tell,
To friends and family dear.
"Wrap me!" he cried.
She quickly grabbed a blanket from the bed.
As good Khadeejah listened well to what the angel said.

Said wise Khadeejah tenderly,
"Who else would Allah choose?
You speak the truth. You're fair to all.
You speak the truth. You're fair to all.
You surely cannot lose.
Your kindness, generosity, and name are known to all.
To you alone, Muhammad, Allah would surely call."

Muhammad was now the Prophet of Allah,
Rasoolullah

Listen to this Nasheed on Track 11 of your CD.

Think Critically

Why do you think Allah chose Muhammad ﷺ even though he could not read or write?

healthy
habit

Always have some time to be alone at home or in the masjid to read Qur'an. Say thikr, or make du'aa.

Study Questions

1 When and where did Muhammad ﷺ become a prophet?

2 Who visited Prophet Muhammad ﷺ in the cave?

3 What did the visitor do or say to Muhammad ﷺ? And what did Muhammad say to him?

4 What were the first ayat revealed to the Prophet ﷺ?

5 How did Khadeejah help Prophet Muhammad ﷺ?

6 What are the proper manners of sitting in the masjid?

MUHAMMAD, RASOOLULLAH, TEACHES HIS FAMILY AND FRIENDS

Questions?

1. Who were the first people to become Muslims?
2. Why did these people believe in Rasoolullah?
3. What is a Sahabi?
4. What do we say when we mention or hear the name of a Sahabi?

Main Idea: Learn some basic facts about the first Muslims.

Word Watch

Sahabi	صحابي
Sahaba	صحابة
Sahabiyyah	صحابية
Sahabiyyat	صحابيات
Radiya-Allahu Anhu	رضي الله عنه
Radiya-Allahu Anha	رضي الله عنها

Muhammad ﷺ became **Rasoolullah**. What does "Rasoolullah" mean?

Rasoolullah means the Messenger of Allah. This is the one who delivers the message from Allah ﷻ to the people.

The children were excited. They were waiting in the masjid to hear the Seerah of Prophet Muhammad ﷺ. They prayed in the masjid and finished their Sunnah prayer. Teacher Luqman took a little bit longer to complete his Sunnah prayer.

Luqman: Assalamu alaikum.

Group: Wa alaikum as-Salam wa Rahmatullahi wa barakatuh.

Luqman: Are you ready to start our lesson today?

Bilal: Yes, we can't wait.

Luqman: All right. We learned last time that Muhammad ﷺ was chosen by Allah to be the final messenger to all mankind. His mission was to teach Islam to all people.

RASOOLULLAH TEACHES HIS FAMILY

Prophet Muhammad ﷺ began teaching Islam to his family and relatives.

- The first woman to believe in him was his wife Khadeejah رضي الله عنها.
- The first man was his friend Abu Bakr رضي الله عنه.
- The first boy to believe in the Prophet was his cousin Ali.
- The first servant was Zaid bin Harithah.

Many more of the Prophet's friends and family believed in him and became Muslims. They believed that Allah was the One and Only God. They also believed in all the prophets who were sent by Allah, starting with Adam عليه السلام and ending with Muhammad ﷺ.

There are many others who accepted Islam early on. They were Othman Ibn Affan, Sa'd Ibn abi Waqqas, Az-Zubayr Ibn-ul-Awwam, Talhah Ibn Obaydillah, Sa'eed Ibn Zaid, Obaydah Ibn Jarrah, and others.

Q. WHAT IS A "SAHABI?"

A. A sahabi is a man who saw the Prophet ﷺ and believed in him. We should say: "Radiy-Allahu anhu" رضي الله عنه after we say or hear his name. Sahabah is the plural of sahabi.

Q. HOW ABOUT IF IT WAS A WOMAN?

A. We call her a Sahabiyyah. We should say: "Radiya-Allahu anha" رضي الله عنها which means "May Allah be pleased with her" after we say or hear her name. Sahabiyyat is the plural of sahabiyyah.

ABU BAKR AS-SIDDEEQ (R)

أبو بـكـر الصـديق رضي الله عنه

Abu Bakr As-Siddeeq رضي الله عنه was a very close friend of Prophet Muhammad ﷺ. Abu Bakr was the first man to accept Islam. When Abu Bakr became a Muslim, he told other people about Islam. He also helped Islam by freeing many Muslim slaves. Abu Bakr was a very generous man, and he used all of his money to help Islam and Muslims. Prophet Muhammad ﷺ picked Abu Bakr to travel with him to Madinah.

On the way to Madinah, the Prophet ﷺ rested in a cave called Thaur. In the cave, the Prophet slept on Abu Bakr's lap. A scorpion stung Abu Bakr, but he did not move or make any noise because he did not want to disturb the Prophet. Abu Bakr loved the Prophet more than he loved himself!

Abu Bakr was known as As-Siddeeq, which means the truthful, and the one who believes.

After the Prophet ﷺ died, Abu Bakr became the leader of all Muslims, and the first Khaleefah of Islam. He was promised by Allah to go to Jannah. Abu Bakr passed away in Madinah two years after the passing of Prophet Muhammad ﷺ. He was sixty-three years old. He was buried next to Prophet Muhammad ﷺ.

OMAR IBN AL-KHATTAB (R)

عمـر ابن الخـطاب رضي الله عنه

Omar ibn Al-Khattab رضي الله عنه was known to be one of the strongest and most fearless men, before and after he embraced Islam. At that time, Muslims were few and weak.

Once, Prophet Muhammad ﷺ made a du'aa':

"Oh Allah! Make Islam strong with either of two men, Amr bin Hisham (Abu Jahl), or Omar bin Khattab."

The prayer was answered. Allah guided Omar to serve Islam. Omar was a great pillar of strength for Islam. Omar had great virtue. Omar was also very pious and sincere. He used to cry during salah. He was always afraid of Allah.

Omar was greatly educated and knowledgeable. He had learned to read and write while still a child, a very rare thing in Makkah at the time.

When he became the second Khaleefah of Islam after Abu Bakr, Omar spent many nights going around the streets of Madinah to see whether any-one needed help. Omar was fair, strong, and right-eous during his ten years as a Khaleefah. He was promised by Allah to go to Jannah. He passed away when he was sixty-three years old. He was buried next to the Prophet ﷺ and Abu Bakr.

UTHMAN IBN AFFAN (R)

عثمان ابن عــفــان رضي الله عنه

Uthman ibn Affan رضي الله عنه embraced Islam at the very early time of Islam. He was wealthy and generous. Prophet Muhammad ﷺ said:

"... the most truthful in his modesty is Uthman."

He was so modest that even the angels felt shy before him. The Prophet Muhammad ﷺ said:

"Shall I not feel shy before a man when even the angels feel shy before him?"

Uthman ibn Affan was very pious. He used to read much of the Qur'an and stand for hours during prayer. Once he stood before a grave and cried until his beard was wet.

Uthman ibn Affan was the third Khaleefah in Islam. He was Khaleefah for 12 years. He was promised by Allah to go to Jannah.

His nick-name was "Thon-Noorayn," which means, "The One Who Has Two Lights," because he was married to two of Prophet Muhammad's daughters.

'ALI IBN ABI TALIB (R)

على ابن أبي طالب رضي الله عنه

'Ali Ibn Abi Talib رضي الله عنه was the first child to accept Islam. He was ten years old when the Prophet told his family about Islam. 'Ali is the cousin of the Prophet. His father's name was Abu Talib. Abu Talib was the uncle of the Prophet.

The Prophet ﷺ once said:

"I am the City of Knowledge, and 'Ali is its gate."

'Ali رضي الله عنه was known for his great knowledge and wisdom. 'Ali was also a great warrior on the battle-field, and he never lost in a single war.

'Ali married Fatimah, who was the daughter of the Prophet ﷺ. 'Ali later became the fourth Khaleefah in Islam. He was Khaleefah for about six years.

'Ali ibn Abi Talib is a great role model. He accepted Islam when he was very young! He never worshipped idols, or anything other than Allah.

He was promised by Allah to go to Jannah.

ACTIVITY time

Make a poster about five great sahabah. Write their names and one paragraph about each one of them.

healthy habit

1. Always say "Radiy-Allahu anhu" after you say or hear the name of the sahabi or sahabiyyah.
2. Always follow the great manners of as-sahabah.

Study Questions

Who was the first man to exapt islam

1. What did Khadeejah tell Prophet Muhammad to do?

First man

2. What was his response?

3. Who was the first person to become Muslim? First man? First child?

4. What is a sahabi? Name a few sahabah.

Questions?

1. How did the leaders of Quraysh hurt the early Muslims?
2. How did the Muslims act when they were suffering?
3. Why did the early Muslims keep their faith?
4. What was the reward for their patience?
5. Where did the Muslims go to look for safety?

Main Idea: True Muslims will keep faith and never leave their religion, even when they are under pressure.

Word Watch

Shirk	شِرك
Kuffar	كفار
Kafir	كافر
Ahad	أحد
Abyssinia	الحبشة
As-Saboor	الصبور
Asnam (Idols)	أصنام
An-Najashi	النَّجاشى

Abu Jahl	أبو جهل
Umayyah Ibn Khalaf	أمية ابن خلف
Sumayyah	سُـمية
Yasir	يـاسر
Ammar Ibn Yasir	عمار ابن يـاسر
Abdullah Ibn Mas'ood	عبدالله ابن مسعود
Bilal ibn Rabah	بلال ابن رباح

THOSE WHO DID NOT BELIEVE

Teacher Luqman looked a little unhappy when he was teaching this part of the story of Rasoolullah ﷺ.

Teacher Luqman: When the Prophet ﷺ started teaching Islam, few people believed him and became Muslims. Sadly, most of the people did not believe in Islam.

People in Makkah used to worship idols and statues. They had about 360 idols (Asnam أصنام) around and inside Al-Ka'bah. They thought that worshipping these gods would bring them closer to Allah ﷻ . This is called "Shirk," which means worshipping false gods, or anything other than Allah.

This is the worst sin a person can commit.

I AM HERE TO HELP YOU

Prophet Muhammad ﷺ explained to the people of Makkah that he was there to help them learn what Allah wants from them. He told them that if they worshipped Allah alone and did good deeds, they would win Al-Jannah, or Paradise. But if they insisted on worshipping idols, and doing bad deeds, they would be punished in Jahannam, or Hellfire. Many of them laughed at Rasoolullah and refused to follow Islam. They told him that their fathers and grandfathers had taught them to worship the idols, and they knew better than he did. They told him that they would not leave the religion of their ancestors.

Bilal: This is bad. Rasoolullah wanted them to go to Jannah, and they wanted to go to Jahannam.

Teacher Luqman: That is sad, isn't it?

Group: Yes!

ABU JAHL, THE FATHER OF IGNORANCE

Teacher Luqman: One of the worst enemies of Islam was a man called Amr ibn Hisham. He used to abuse and kill or hurt people who became Muslims. He thought they would leave Islam if he bothered them. Quraysh used to call him "Abul Hakam," which means the "Father of Wisdom." But because he refused to believe in Islam, the Prophet ﷺ called him "Abu Jahl," which means the "Father of Ignorance." Abu Jahl was the worst kafir in Makkah.

Ahmad: He deserved that!

Teacher Luqman: Prophet Muhammad ﷺ tried his best to convince him to become a Muslim. He invited Abu Jahl to Islam many, many times, but he refused.

Zaid: Why in the world would the disbelievers do such a thing? They worshipped stones, not Allah, the One Who created them.

Teacher Luqman: Abu Jahl and other leaders knew that Muhammad was truthful. But they were afraid that if they followed him, they would lose their place as leaders. Their leadership was more important to them than pleasing Allah.

YASIR FAMILY: JANNAH IS YOUR HOME

Teacher Luqman: Let's go on. Abu Jahl and a group of his friends got angry when the family of Yasir became Muslims. Yasir ياسر , his wife Sumayyah سُمية , and their son Ammar Ibn Yasir عمار ابن ياسر , all accepted Islam. Abu Jahl wanted them to leave Islam and worship his idols, but of course they refused. Abu Jahl tortured all of them in a very harsh way. The Prophet ﷺ tried to stop Abu Jahl and his people, but couldn't. So he spoke to the family of Yasir and said:

"صبرا آل ياسر فإنَّ موعدكم الـجنَّة"

"Be patient, Family of Yasir. You are promised Paradise. "

Later, Yasir and Sumayyah died from the harsh torture. Yasir and Sumayyah showed that they were strong Muslims, and they passed away as Shuhadaa' (martyrs). Ammar did not die, and he insisted to remain a Muslim.

Zaid: That is so sad. Who killed them?

Teacher Luqman: Abu Jahl did.

Bilal: How old were they?

Teacher Luqman: They were about 70 years old.

Ahmad: That is really cruel! How could they kill old people?

AHAD! AHAD!

Bilal: My dad told me that he named me Bilal because he loves the sahabi صحابي Bilal ibn Rabah. He, too, was tortured by the people of Makkah.

Teacher Luqman: Your father did a good thing when he named you after this great sahabi. Bilal Ibn Rabah was a slave in Makkah to a man called Umayyah ibn Khalaf. He was from Abyssinia in Africa. Umayyah used to beat Bilal after he became a Muslim. On hot days, Umayyah took Bilal to the desert and laid him down on the very hot sand. They would whip him so hard. Sometimes Umayyah would order that a big rock be put on his chest. Bilal had a strong belief in Allah and kept on saying:

أحــد أحــد

"Ahad, Ahad!" meaning "Allah is one! Allah is one!"

Abu Bakr felt very sad when he saw Bilal having such a hard time. He begged Umayyah to stop beating Bilal, but Ummayyah refused. So Abu Bakr offered to buy Bilal and his mother Hamamah. Umayyah agreed, but he asked a very high price. Abu Bakr accepted and bought Bilal and his mother with his own money. He set them free. Later, Bilal became the Prophet's mu'athin (the one who calls for the Prayer).

Did you know ...

Abu Bakr freed at least ten slaves in Makkah with his own money. They were tortured by their masters because they became Muslims.

WORDS OF WISDOM
(Hadeeth Shareef)

حديث شريف

Narrated By Muslim

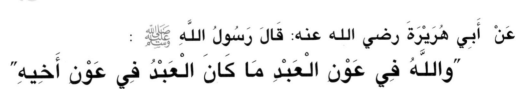

عَنْ أَبِي هُرَيْرَةَ رضي الله عنه: قَالَ رَسُولُ اللَّه ﷺ :

"وَاللَّهُ فِي عَوْنِ الْعَبْدِ مَا كَانَ الْعَبْدُ فِي عَوْنِ أَخِيهِ"

TRANSLITERATION

Wallahu fee 'awn-il-'abdi ma kan-al-'abdu fee awni akheeh

MEANING TRANSLATION

Abu Hurayrah رضي الله عنه reported that Rasoolullah ﷺ said: "Allah will help his servant, as long as he helps his brother."

The Ear of Abdullah Ibn Mas'ood

Teacher Luqman: Here is another story about the suffering of the first Muslims.

Abdullah Ibn Mas'ood was one of the great sahabah. He had a beautiful voice, and he used to read Al-Qur'an in a very beautiful way. One time, he wanted the people of Makkah to hear the words of Allah. He went to Al-Ka'bah and started to read the Qur'an in a loud voice. The kuffar (disbleivers) of Quraysh did not like that Abu Jahl and other kuffar jumped on Abdullah and beat him up. Abu Jahl, who was always the cruelest, chopped off Abdullah's ear. Abdullah Ibn Mas'ood survived. Even though he suffered a great loss, Abdullah Ibn Mas'ood continued to be a very good Muslim.

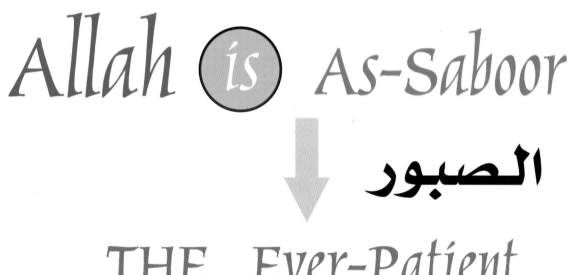

Allah (is) As-Saboor

الصبور

THE Ever-Patient

Allah is so patient with those who disobey him. Good Muslims learn patience from Allah. But they cannot be as patient as Allah is.

WORDS OF WISDOM
Holy Qur'an

سورة الهمزة

Surah Al-Humaza 104: 1-9

بِسْمِ اللَّهِ الرَّحْمَٰنِ الرَّحِيمِ

وَيْلٌ لِّكُلِّ هُمَزَةٍ لُّمَزَةٍ ﴿١﴾ الَّذِي جَمَعَ مَالًا وَعَدَّدَهُ ﴿٢﴾ يَحْسَبُ أَنَّ مَالَهُ أَخْلَدَهُ ﴿٣﴾ كَلَّا لَيُنبَذَنَّ فِي الْحُطَمَةِ ﴿٤﴾ وَمَا أَدْرَاكَ مَا الْحُطَمَةُ ﴿٥﴾ نَارُ اللَّهِ الْمُوقَدَةُ ﴿٦﴾ الَّتِي تَطَّلِعُ عَلَى الْأَفْئِدَةِ ﴿٧﴾ إِنَّهَا عَلَيْهِم مُّؤْصَدَةٌ ﴿٨﴾ فِي عَمَدٍ مُّمَدَّدَةٍ ﴿٩﴾

TRANSLITERATION

[1] Waylul-likulli humazatil lumazah
[2] Allathee jama'a malaw wa'addadah
[3] Ya hsabu anna malahu akhladah
[4] Kalla layunbathanna fil-hutamah
[5] Wama adraka mal hutamah
[6] Nar-ullah-il-mooqadah
[7] Allatee tattali'u alal-af'idah
[8] lnnaha 'alayhim-mu'sadah
[9] Fee 'amadim-mumaddadah

MEANING TRANSLATION

Woe to every backbiter, derider (1) Who accumulates wealth and counts it. (2) He thinks that his wealth has made him eternal. (3) Never! He will certainly be thrown into the Crushing Fire. (4) And what may let you know what the Crushing Fire is? (5) It is Allah's kindled fire (6) That will peep into the hearts. (7) It will be closed on them, (8)In outstretched columns. (9)

Listen to this Sura on Track 13 of your CD.

D34

THE JOURNEY TO ABYSSINIA
AND THE FAIR KING

Zaid: What did Rasoolullah and the Muslims do after they had all of these problems? Did they fight back?

Teacher Luqman: No, the Prophet did not want to fight his people. He and the Muslims were patient. They hoped that the people of Makkah would change their minds and become Muslims one day.

Ahmad: But they were going through very hard times.

Teacher Luqman: That is why the Prophet looked for ways to protect the Muslims. Prophet Muhammad ﷺ did not want his followers to suffer anymore. So, he sent Ja'far Ibn Abi Talib جعفر ابن أبي طالب , Abu Salamah أبو سلمة , and many others to Abyssinia, in East Africa. The king of Abyssinia, Negus (**An-Najashi**), was Christian. He was a kind and fair king. The Prophet ﷺ knew that Muslims would be treated well there. Eighty men, with their wives and children, left to Abyssinia.

The kuffar of Makkah did not like this. They wanted the Muslims to be brought back to Makkah so that they could torture them. So the tribe of Quraysh sent two of their leaders to Abyssinia to bring the Muslims back to Makkah.

When they arrived to Abyssinia, they asked the king to arrest the Muslims and send them back to Makkah. Because An-Najashi was a fair king he refused to arrest them or send them back. He allowed the Muslims to stay in his country as long as they wanted. In fact, An-Najashi himself later became a Muslim.

We have learned...

❶   The early Muslims showed great love to Allah (SWT), even though they were hurt.

❷   We should not give up on what we believe in.

❸   Allah ﷻ tests us to see how strong our iman is.

❹   Abu Jahl was one of the worst enemies of Islam.

❺   Muslims left Makkah and went to Abyssinia for the sake of Allah.

ACTIVITY time

Sit in a group of five students and answer this question:

If you were in Bilal's situation, what would you do?

STAND UP FOR ISLAM

We believe in only One God,
And His Name is Allah.
He created us to worship Him and say "Insha Allah."
(chorus)

La ilaha ilallah, Muslims say it loudly.
La ilaha ilallah, stand up for Islam proudly.

A Muslim prays five times a day, but first must do his wudoo'.
We wash our hands and face and arms, and in between our
toes, too.
(chorus)

A Muslim fasts in Ramadan, from dawn until the sunset.
We dress in our best clothes on Eid, and dream of presents
we'll get.
(chorus)

A Muslim gives zakat to help the poor and help the needy,
Teaching us to share with others all,
and not be greedy.
(chorus)

A Muslim must go on the Hajj at least once in his lifetime.
Going round the house of Allah, not just once, but seven
times.
(chorus)

Listen to this nasheed on Track 14 of your CD.

Islam in Ethiopia

Ethiopia is the new name for Abyssinia. It is a country in East Africa. As you learned earlier, Islam arrived early in Ethiopia. Prophet Muhammad sent about eighty of the early Muslims to this land so they would not be tortured by the kuffar of Makkah. These early Muslims were good and decent people. The Ethiopians liked and trusted them. That made many East Afican people accept Islam. Even the king of ancient Ethiopia believed in Muhammad, and he became a Muslim. His name was Negus Armah, or in Arabic, An-Najashi. He protected Muslims there and treated them with kindness. When he died, Prophet Muhammad ﷺ did salatul janazah (the Funeral Prayer) on his soul. Now, nearly half of the people in Ethiopia are Muslims.

The capital of Ethiopia is Adis Ababa.

Think Critically

1. Why do you think the idol worshippers of Makkah did not try to kill or torture Prophet Muhammad or Abu Bakr in the beginning?

2. Make a connection between the trip of Muslims to Abyssinia and a Sahabi. The Muslims who went to his native land were safe there, but he was tortured in Makkah. Who is this Sahabi?

Study  Questions

1. Did all the people of Makkah become Muslims at the beginning of Islam? Why?

2. Who was Abu Jahl? What did he do to the Muslims? Give some examples.

3. Why did the leaders of Makkah torture the first Muslims?

4. What did the Prophet and early Muslims do to protect themselves from the kuffar of Makkah?

5. Write the names of five early Muslims who were tortured by the kuffar of Makkah.

6. Write a paragraph on Islam in Ethiopia.

Prophet Muhammad Was Strong And Patient

Questions?

1. What is patience?
2. What can you do to control your anger?
3. How did the Prophet ﷺ act toward his enemies?
4. What did the Quraysh offer the Prophet ﷺ if he would stop spreading the message of Islam?
5. What was the Prophet's answer to the Quraysh?

Main Idea: We should learn from the Prophet's example to be patient and strong, even in the face of hard times.

Word

Sabr ((Patience)	صبر
Fortune Teller	كاهن
Poet	شاعر
Dunya	دُنيا
Akhirah	آخرة

Q. Do you know what patience means?

A. **Patience** is controlling oneself, and being calm even when things are not going smoothly. A Muslim must learn to accept that sometimes life's challenges are a test from Allah. If we make du'aa' and show **sabr** (patience), Allah will help us and reward us.

ABU LAHAB AND HIS WIFE

Prophet Muhammad ﷺ had great patience. He knew that people would try to harm him in Makkah. But he waited, hoping that they would believe in Allah (SWT). He did not give up on them.

Rasoolullah ﷺ had many uncles. Some of them accepted Islam, like Hamzah رضي الله عنه and Al-Abbas رضي الله عنه . Others did not become Muslims, like Abu Lahab. Abu Lahab's wife, Ummu Jameel, wanted to harm the Prophet ﷺ like her husband did. She snuck out at night in front of the Prophet's house and left thorny branches at the door. In the morning, when the Prophet ﷺ left home early, he would step on the thorns and hurt his feet. Rasoolullah stayed calm and showed patience.

Allah ﷻ saw what happened, and He promised that He would punish Abu Lahab and his wife. Let's read together the surah that talks about them:

﴿ تَبَّتْ يَدَا أَبِي لَهَبٍ وَتَبَّ ۝ مَا أَغْنَىٰ عَنْهُ مَالُهُ وَمَا كَسَبَ ۝ سَيَصْلَىٰ نَارًا ذَاتَ لَهَبٍ ۝ وَامْرَأَتُهُ حَمَّالَةَ الْحَطَبِ ۝ فِي جِيدِهَا حَبْلٌ مِّن مَّسَدٍ ۝ ﴾

Perish the two hands of Abu Lahab, and perish he! (1) Neither his wealth benefited him, nor what he earned. (2)He will soon enter a Fire, full of flames, (3) And his wife as well,___the wicked carrier of firewood. (4) Around her neck, there is (a collar of iron, like) a well-twisted rope. 5 (5)
Surah Al-Masadd 111: 1-5

Listen to this Surah on Track 15 of your CD.

THE QURAYSH FIGHT ISLAM

The Quraysh did not want Islam to spread in Makkah. They wanted to continue worshipping idols (asnam). That was the religion of their fathers and grandfathers. They had many evil plans to stop the Prophet ﷺ from spreading his message.

Plan  Calling the Prophet Names

The Quraysh and the people in Makkah called the Prophet many bad names. They thought that by doing this they would make people hate him and turn away from his message. They called him crazy and said that he was a liar. When people started to hear the Qur'an and like it, they called the prophet a poet (someone who writes poems) and a "fortune teller" (someone who tells the future). They even called him a sorcerer (magician). People knew that the Prophet was none of these things. They knew that the Prophet ﷺ was an honest and truthful man, and that the leaders of Quraysh were lying. They themselves used to call him "Assadiqul Ameen" (the Honest and the Trustworthy) before he became a prophet. But they made up all of these bad names just to stop him from teaching Islam.

Plan  Let's Make a Deal: Worship Our idols and Your God Together.

The leaders of Quraysh found that the insults were not making Muhammad ﷺ stop teaching Islam. They needed a new plan. They decided to try to make a deal with the Prophet. The Quraysh told Rasoolullah ﷺ that they would worship Allah ﷻ some of the time, and he would have to worship their gods sometimes. The Prophet ﷺ did not agree to this plan. Prophet Muhammad and true Muslims would never worship anyone or anything except God ﷻ .

Plan  Making Generous Offers

The Quraysh came to Abu Talib, the Prophet's uncle, to speak with him and try to change his mind. They offered to give the Prophet ﷺ a lot of money and to make him their leader. In return, they wanted Prophet Muhammad ﷺ to stop teaching Islam. Rasoolullah did not accept this bribe.

Abu Talib was not a Muslim, but unlike Abu Lahab, he was very kind to the Prophet. He warned Prophet Muhammad that the Quraysh might try to harm him if he did not make a deal with them. But the Prophet ﷺ did not change his mind.

He gave his uncle Abu Talib the famous answer:

"My uncle, if they were to put the sun in my right hand and the moon in my left hand to stop me from preaching Islam, I would never stop. I will keep inviting people to Islam until I die."

Abu Talib knew that his nephew Muhammad ﷺ was delivering Allah's message, and that he was patient. Abu Talib said:
"My nephew, say what you like and do whatever you want. By Allah, I will never leave you alone."

Plan  Kill the Prophet

The leaders of Makkah were shocked when the Prophet ﷺ refused their offers. They came again to Abu Talib and complained about his nephew. They said that Muhammad ﷺ was still saying bad things about their religion and their gods. They offered to give Abu Talib one of the best young men of the Quraysh to adopt as his son. In return, they wanted to take Muhammad ﷺ. Abu Talib knew that their plan was to kill Muhammad ﷺ, so he refused.

WORDS OF WISDOM

Holy Qur'an

سورة الطارق

Surah At-Tariq 86: 1-17

بِسْمِ اللَّهِ الرَّحْمَٰنِ الرَّحِيمِ

وَٱلسَّمَآءِ وَٱلطَّارِقِ ﴿١﴾ وَمَآ أَدْرَىٰكَ مَا ٱلطَّارِقُ ﴿٢﴾ ٱلنَّجْمُ ٱلثَّاقِبُ ﴿٣﴾ إِن كُلُّ نَفْسٍ لَّمَّا عَلَيْهَا حَافِظٌ ﴿٤﴾ فَلْيَنظُرِ ٱلْإِنسَٰنُ مِمَّ خُلِقَ ﴿٥﴾ خُلِقَ مِن مَّآءٍ دَافِقٍ ﴿٦﴾ يَخْرُجُ مِنۢ بَيْنِ ٱلصُّلْبِ وَٱلتَّرَآئِبِ ﴿٧﴾ إِنَّهُۥ عَلَىٰ رَجْعِهِۦ لَقَادِرٌ ﴿٨﴾ يَوْمَ تُبْلَى ٱلسَّرَآئِرُ ﴿٩﴾ فَمَا لَهُۥ مِن قُوَّةٍ وَلَا نَاصِرٍ ﴿١٠﴾ وَٱلسَّمَآءِ ذَاتِ ٱلرَّجْعِ ﴿١١﴾ وَٱلْأَرْضِ ذَاتِ ٱلصَّدْعِ ﴿١٢﴾ إِنَّهُۥ لَقَوْلٌ فَصْلٌ ﴿١٣﴾ وَمَا هُوَ بِٱلْهَزْلِ ﴿١٤﴾ إِنَّهُمْ يَكِيدُونَ كَيْدًا ﴿١٥﴾ وَأَكِيدُ كَيْدًا ﴿١٦﴾ فَمَهِّلِ ٱلْكَٰفِرِينَ أَمْهِلْهُمْ رُوَيْدًۢا ﴿١٧﴾

TRANSLITERATION

[1] Wassamaa'i wattariq
[2] Wama adraaka mattariq
[3] Annajm-uth-thaqib
[4] In kullu nafsil-lamma 'alayha hafith
[5] Falyanthur-il-insaanu mimma khuliq
[6] Khuliqa mim-maa-'in dafiq
[7] Yakhruju mim-bayn-is-sulbi wattaraa'ib
[8] Innahu 'ala raj'ihi-laqadir
[9] Yawma tubla-ssaraa'ir
[10] Fama lahu min quwwatiw-wala nasir
[11] Wassama'i that-ir-raj'i
[12] Wal-'ardi that-is-sad'i

[13] Innahu laqawlun fasl
[14] Wama huwa bilhazl
[15] Innahum yakeedoona kayda
[16] Wa'akeedu kayda
[17] Famahhil-il-kafireena amhilhum ruwayda

MEANING TRANSLATION

I swear by the sky and by the Night-Comer, (1) And what may let you know what the Night-Comer is? (2) The star of piercing brightness! (3) There is no human being, but there is a watcher over him. (4) So, let man consider of which stuff he is created. (5) He is created of spouting water (6) That comes out from between the loins and the chest-bones. (7) Surely He is Powerful to bring him back (8) On a day when all the secrets will be searched out, (9) And he will have neither strength (to defend), nor a supporter. (10) I swear by the sky that rains, (11) And the earth that cracks open (for plants), (12) This is a decisive word, (13) And it is not a joke. (14) They are devising plans, (15) And I Am devising plans. (16) So leave the disbelievers alone at the moment; give them respite for a while. (17)

What did we learn from this?

1 Allah سبحانه وتعالى is with those who are patient.

2 Prophet Muhammad ﷺ showed a great deal of patience.

3 The Prophet ﷺ practiced patience with the Quraysh and did not give up his mission.

Allah (is) Al-Muntaqim
THE Avenger المنتقم

He punishes the evil people and helps the believers to prevail over them.

 time

Practicing Patience
Write a short paragraph on how you would act in each of the following situations.
1. Your little sister spilled juice on the homework that you just completed.
2. Your soccer team lost the game.
3. Your friend called you a rude name.
4. You asked your parents for a special game, and they told you they could not afford it.

Think Critically

1. We learned that Abu Talib loved and protected Prophet Muhammad. Why do you think Abu Talib did not become Muslim?
2. How do you think Prophet Muhammad felt about Abu Talib not accepting Islam?

Study  Questions

1 What was the name of the uncle of the Prophet who used to hurt him? What was his wife's name? What did she used to do?

2 What names did the Quraysh call the Prophet ﷺ? What would you do if someone called you bad names?

3 What was the deal that the leaders of the Quraysh offered the prophet?

4 How did the leaders of Quraysh try to kill Muhammad ﷺ?

The Boycott Against The Muslims

Questions?

1. Why do you think the Quraysh wanted to hurt the Prophet?
2. What do you think they would do to stop him from teaching people Islam? How far would they go?
3. What do you think the Prophet did? Did he stop teaching Islam, or did he continue to teach? Do you think he made the right decision?

Main Idea: The Quraysh boycotted the family of the Prophet and Muslims for protecting Prophet Muhammad. They hoped that this would force the Muslims to stop believing.

Word Watch

Boycott	مقاطعة
As-Saheefah	الصَّحيفة
Bani Hashim	بَني هاشم
The Year of Sorrow	عام الـحُزن

Q. Do you know what a **boycott** is?

A. To **boycott** means to completely avoid someone. When someone is being boycotted, others will not trade with him. They will not sell him goods or buy goods from him.

The kuffar in Makkah had been torturing the Muslims to make them worship idols again. This did not work. There were more people becoming Muslims all the time. Hamzah, the uncle of Rasoolullah, and Omar ibn-ul-Khattab, who were both very important men in Makkah, had become Muslims.

The chiefs of the Quraysh were becoming very worried. They were afraid that Rasoolullah and the Muslims would take over Makkah. They asked Abu Talib and Banu Hashim, the family of the Prophet, to give Muhammad ﷺ to the leaders of the Quraysh so that they could kill him. Bani Hashim refused. The chiefs of the Quraysh decided to act very harshly against Bani Hashim and the Muslims.

All of these leaders signed an agreement against the Muslims. This agreement said that all the people of Makkah must boycott Bani Hashim and all the Muslims. No one in Makkah was allowed to talk to them, marry them, buy their goods, or sell anything to them. The kuffar even prevented anyone from giving food or medicine to Muslims.

They wrote this evil agreement on a piece of leather and hung it inside Al-Ka'bah. The chiefs made a promise that every one of them would respect this agreement. They called it As-Saheefah, which means "the page."

Prophet Muhammad ﷺ and the Muslims had to move to a small valley in Makkah owned by Abu Talib, the Prophet's uncle.

The Prophet ﷺ, Muslims, and the Prophet's relatives were suffering from the boycott. They did not have enough food or clothing. They could not buy anything or sell anything. Muslims had to stay for days without food. They even had to eat tree leaves and rotten food to stay alive. They became weak and sick. Khadeejah رضي الله عنها, the Prophet's wife, became very ill.

Three years passed, and the Muslims continued to suffer. Finally, five chiefs of the Quraysh began feeling unhappy with what they'd done. "What are we doing to our old friends and neighbors?" they asked. They knew that the boycott was cruel. They told Abu Jahl and other chiefs of Makkah that they would tear up the agreement and end the boycott. Abu Jahl and the rest of the leaders refused. The chiefs started to argue among themselves until Abu Talib came.

He said that Muhammad ﷺ had told him something very strange. Allah revealed to Muhammad ﷺ that termites had destroyed the written agreement inside Al-Ka'bah. "Look!" Abu Talib said to Abu Jahl and the chiefs of the Quraysh. "If we open the door of Al-Ka'bah and find that Muhammad was wrong, I will give him up to you. But if we find that what he said is true, then he is a Prophet and you must end this boy-cott." The chiefs agreed. They went inside Al-Ka'bah and found the leather parchment eaten up! It was all gone except for the one line that read: " باسمك اللهم By Your Name, O Allah." The five chiefs said: "We must stop this boycott." The other Quraysh chiefs had to agree. They knew there would be a war in Makkah if they did not.

The Prophet ﷺ and his followers and relatives finally went home. Everyone was weak and exhausted. They had shown perseverance in their belief in Allah and He had supported them.

The boycott was over and they had proven that they would never change their religion.

healthy

habit

Always try to make sure you are doing the right thing. And keep pleasing Allah, even if it is difficult sometimes. This is the way to get great hasanat and win a high level in Jannah.

عامُ الـحُزْن

THE YEAR OF
SORROW

Shortly after the boycott was over, in the tenth year of prophet-hood, a sad thing happened. Khadeejah, the Prophet's wife, and Abu Talib, the Prophet's uncle, both died. Both died in the same year, so Muslims called it "The Year of Sorrow عامُ الـحُزن ."

Khadeejah was more than just a wife to Prophet Muhammad ﷺ. She was his best friend. She gave him love and strength. She was one of the greatest women in Islam. In fact, she was the first person to become a Muslim after Rasoolullah ﷺ.
The Prophet ﷺ was sad.

Abu Talib also was dear to Prophet Muhammad ﷺ. He was like a father to him. He had always protected and supported him. The saddest thing was that he had not become a Muslim himself. He was afraid that if he accepted Islam, Abu Jahl and the chiefs of Quraysh would speak badly about him after his death. Rasoolullah ﷺ tried his best to help him accept Islam, but Abu Talib refused.

Muslims Continue to Suffer

After the death of Khadeejah and Abu Talib, the unbelievers became harsher against Muslims. Without Abu Talib's protection, they felt that they could easily hurt Muhammad ﷺ.

After the death of Abu Talib, the Prophet ﷺ faced new challenges because he was perceived as being weak. But strong and important people continued to accept Islam and protect it.

One time the unbelievers threw dirt on Prophet Muhammad ﷺ. The Prophet ﷺ went home, and his daughter Fatimah washed his head. She cried: "The people are being too cruel!"

The Prophet ﷺ replied: "Do not cry, my daughter, for Allah will defend your father."

Another time, the Prophet ﷺ was praying beside Al-Ka'ba. A chief of the Quraysh found him. The chief's name was Uqbah ibn Abi Mu'ayt. He tried to strangle the Prophet ﷺ. Abu Bakr was walking by and saw what happened. He grabbed Uqbah and threw him down. He yelled, "You would kill a man just because he says 'Allah is my Lord?'"

The Quraysh continued trying to hurt the Prophet ﷺ and stop Islam.

Think Critically

Based on the story in this lesson, who do you think gained the most from the boycott, the kuffar of the Quraysh or the Muslims? Why?

 Study  Questions

1. Why did the chiefs of the Quraysh want to boycott the Muslims?

2. What does boycott mean?

3. How did the boycott affect the Muslims?

4. What was the Quraysh's agreement called in Arabic?

5. What did Allah tell Rasoolullah about the Quraysh's agreement?

6. How did the boycott end?

7. What happened during the tenth year of Prophethood? How did the Prophet feel about it?

8. What did Muslims do when they faced severe and difficult times?

Al-Isra' wal-MI'RAJ: The Heavenly Trip

Questions?

1. Do you think Allah would allow the Prophet and the Muslims to suffer without supporting them?
2. How do you think Allah supported His prophet?

Word Watch

Al-Isra'	الإسراء
Al-Mi'raj	المِعراج
Al-Buraq	البُراقْ
Jerusalem	القُدس
Al-Aqsa Mosque	المسجد الأقصى
Rajab	رَجب
Sidrat-ul-Muntaha	سدرة المنتهى

Allah ﷻ knew that Prophet Muhammad ﷺ had suffered long enough. The Prophet went through a lot of hardship for the sake of Allah. Allah wanted to reward His Prophet and ease his suffering. He also wanted to show the Prophet ﷺ how important he was. Allah rewarded the prophet by showing him a great miracle, the miracle of Al-Isra' wal-Mi'raj.

WORDS OF WISDOM
Holy Qur'an

سورة الإسراء

Surah Al-Isra 17: 1

بِسْمِ ٱللَّهِ ٱلرَّحْمَٰنِ ٱلرَّحِيمِ

سُبْحَٰنَ ٱلَّذِىٓ أَسْرَىٰ بِعَبْدِهِۦ لَيْلًا مِّنَ ٱلْمَسْجِدِ ٱلْحَرَامِ إِلَى ٱلْمَسْجِدِ ٱلْأَقْصَا ٱلَّذِى بَٰرَكْنَا حَوْلَهُۥ لِنُرِيَهُۥ مِنْ ءَايَٰتِنَآ إِنَّهُۥ هُوَ ٱلسَّمِيعُ ٱلْبَصِيرُ ﴿١﴾

TRANSLITERATION

Subhan-allathee asra bi'abdihi laylan min-almasjidi-lharami ilal-masjid-il-aqsa-llathee barakna hawlahu linuriyahu min ayatina innahu huwa-ssamee'ul-baseer

MEANING TRANSLATION

Glorious is He Who made his servant travel by night from Al-Masjid-ul-Haram to Al-Masjid-ul-Aqsa whose environs We have blessed, so that We let him see some of Our signs. Surely, He is the All-Hearing, the All- Seeing. (1)

Al-Aqsa Mosque

Dome of the Rock

One night, while the Prophet was sleeping, Angel Jibreel came to him and woke him up. Angel Jibreel brought with him a horse-like creature called "Al-Buraq البُراق."

The Prophet ﷺ rode on Al-Buraq. Very quickly, the Prophet and Angel Jibreel arrived at Al-Aqsa Mosque المسجد الأقصى in Jerusalem, a city in Palestine. The journey from Makkah to Jerusalem القُدس was called "Al-Isra' الإسراء." This journey would normally have taken a month, but Al-Buraq was much faster than horses and camels.

All the prophets of Allah ﷻ were at Al-Aqsa mosque waiting for Prophet Muhammad ﷺ. They had been brought back to life by Allah. Rasoolullah was pleased to meet all the great prophets of Allah, like Adam, Noah, Ibraheem, Isma'eel', Ishaq, Musa, Isa, and many others. Meeting these prophets showed Prophet Muhammad ﷺ that he was part of a very special group of people. They had all been chosen by Allah to serve Him and deliver His message on Earth. Angel Jibreel asked Prophet Muhammad ﷺ to be the imam and lead all the prophets in prayer.

Think about it!

Why do you think Prophet Muhammad was chosen to be the imam of these great prophets in salah?

After the prayer, Angel Jibreel عليه السلام took the Prophet ﷺ to the seventh Heaven. The Prophet saw a special tree there. The name of that tree is Sidratul Muntaha سدرة المُنتهى . On each of its leaves there was an angel praising Allah. At that place also, Rasoolullah ﷺ saw Jibreel in his angel form. Prophet Muhammad ﷺ had seen Jibreel in human form before, but in his angel form, Jibreel was amazing. He had six hundred wings!!

After Sidratul Muntaha سدرة المُنتهى , Angel Jibreel could not go any further. Allah did not permit Jibreel to go any farther, so the Prophet ﷺ went on without him. The Prophet kept going higher and farther until he reached the highest level in the Heavens. Allah, the Most High, allowed him to come very close to His throne, which is so great and high above the seventh Heaven.

How do you think Prophet Muhammad ﷺ felt when he met all of the messengers who came before him?

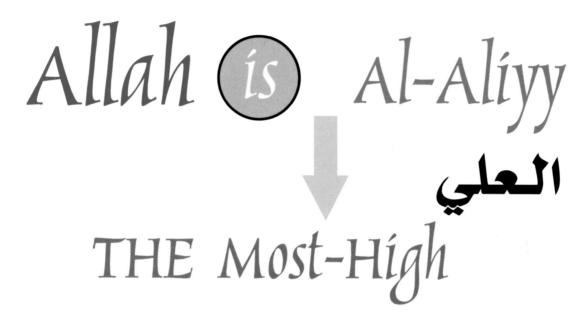

Allah (is) Al-Aliyy

العلي

THE Most-High

He is the highest in power and position above all His creation.

Allah ﷻ granted the Prophet a great welcome. Rasoolullah ﷺ was not able to see Allah, but he saw bright light everywhere. The Prophet ﷺ was very happy and felt great peace in his heart.

The Prophet had seen many wonderful places and things in the Heavens. Before Prophet Muhammad ﷺ left, Allah ordered that Muslims must perform prayers five times a day. Allah said that He would reward those who pray the five daily prayers as if they had prayed fifty prayers. Allah is so generous that He rewards Muslims ten times for each good deed. One prayer is like ten. Five prayers are like fifty.

Allah (is) Al-Kareem

الكريم

THE Generous

Allah showers us with His gifts every day. He also gives us great rewards when we do good deeds. His rewards will help us go to Jannah. Jannah is the greatest gift anyone can get. Allah is Al-Kareem.

Before sunrise, the Prophet ﷺ was brought back to Makkah. His trip from Jerusalem to the Seventh Heaven and beyond is called "Al-Mi'raj المِعراج ." The Journey of Isra' and Mi'raj الإسراء والمِعراج is remembered every year on the 27th day of Rajab رجب ,the seventh month of the Islamic calendar. Some scholars think that this heavenly trip happened on that day.

In the morning, the Prophet ﷺ told his story to the people of Makkah. The non-Muslims did not believe him, and they laughed at him. "How could you have done all of that in just one night?" they asked. "The trip to Jerusalem takes a month by camel. It takes another month to return. Yet you say you also went to Heaven, and you did all of this in one night! You lie!"

They went to Abu Bakr and told him what the Prophet had said. They hoped that Abu Bakr would join them and leave the Prophet. Instead, Abu Bakr said: "If he says that he went on such a journey, I believe him. It must be true."

Abu Bakr and the others went to see the Prophet ﷺ. They wanted him to prove that he was speaking the truth. Abu Bakr had been to Jerusalem before, so he asked the Prophet ﷺ to describe Jerusalem and Al-Masjid Al-Aqsa.

Allah helped the Prophet ﷺ to describe the city and Al-Masjid Al-Aqsa to Abu Bakr and the others. As the Prophet ﷺ described these places, which they knew he'd never seen before the miracle, Abu Bakr kept saying: *"Sadaqta, you are right. I witness that you are the Messenger of Allah."*

After that, Muslims called Abu Bakr "**As-Siddeeq,**" which means the "true believer."

Abu Bakr As-Siddeeq is my hero. He was the first Khaleefah after Rasoolullah. Abu Bakr is a nickname. His full name is **Abddullah Ibn Othman At-Taymiyy.**

The Prophet ﷺ also said he had seen a caravan that was about to reach Makkah. He described how the caravan would look and how far it was from the city. After a short time, the caravan arrived. The caravan looked just like the Prophet had described. Even this miracle did not make Abu Jahl and the Quraysh believe the Prophet.

ACTIVITY time

Make a post card with a collage of pictures of Al-Quds, or Jerusalem, showing Al-Masjid Al-Aqsa, Qubbat-us-Sakkrah, and other holy places. Write the name of the place underneath the pictures.

سورة النجم

Surah An-Najm 53: 1-18

وَٱلنَّجۡمِ إِذَا هَوَىٰ ۝١ مَا ضَلَّ صَاحِبُكُمۡ وَمَا غَوَىٰ ۝٢ وَمَا يَنطِقُ عَنِ ٱلۡهَوَىٰٓ ۝٣ إِنۡ هُوَ إِلَّا وَحۡيٌ يُوحَىٰ ۝٤ عَلَّمَهُۥ شَدِيدُ ٱلۡقُوَىٰ ۝٥ ذُو مِرَّةٍ فَٱسۡتَوَىٰ ۝٦ وَهُوَ بِٱلۡأُفُقِ ٱلۡأَعۡلَىٰ ۝٧ ثُمَّ دَنَا فَتَدَلَّىٰ ۝٨ فَكَانَ قَابَ قَوۡسَيۡنِ أَوۡ أَدۡنَىٰ ۝٩ فَأَوۡحَىٰٓ إِلَىٰ عَبۡدِهِۦ مَآ أَوۡحَىٰ ۝١٠ مَا كَذَبَ ٱلۡفُؤَادُ مَا رَأَىٰٓ ۝١١ أَفَتُمَٰرُونَهُۥ عَلَىٰ مَا يَرَىٰ ۝١٢ وَلَقَدۡ رَءَاهُ نَزۡلَةً أُخۡرَىٰ ۝١٣ عِندَ سِدۡرَةِ ٱلۡمُنتَهَىٰ ۝١٤ عِندَهَا جَنَّةُ ٱلۡمَأۡوَىٰٓ ۝١٥ إِذۡ يَغۡشَى ٱلسِّدۡرَةَ مَا يَغۡشَىٰ ۝١٦ مَا زَاغَ ٱلۡبَصَرُ وَمَا طَغَىٰ ۝١٧ لَقَدۡ رَأَىٰ مِنۡ ءَايَٰتِ رَبِّهِ ٱلۡكُبۡرَىٰٓ ۝١٨

TRANSLITERATION

[1] Wannajmi itha hawa
[2] Ma dalla sahibukum wama ghawa
[3] Wama yantiqu an-il-hawa
[4] In huwa illa wahyun yooha
[5] Allamahu shadeed-ul-quwa
[6] Thu mirratin faistawa
[7] Wahuwa bil-'ofuq-il-'aala
[8] Thumma dana fatadalla
[9] Fakana qaba qawsayni aw adna
[10] Fa'awha il a abdihi ma awha
[11] Ma kathab-alfu'adu ma ra'a
[12] Afatumaroonahu ala ma yara

[13] Walaqad ra'ahu nazlatan okhra
[14] inda sidrat-il-muntaha
[15] indaha jannat-ul-ma'wa
[16] Ith yaghsha-ssidrata ma yaghsha
[17] Ma zagh-al-basaru wama tagha
[18] Laqad ra'a min ayaati rabbih-il-kubra

MEANING TRANSLATION

By the star when it goes down to set, (1) Your fellow (the Holy Prophet (S.A.W)) has neither missed the way, nor did he deviate. (2) He does not speak out of (his own) desire. (3) It is but revelation revealed (to him). (4) It is taught to him by one (angel) of strong faculties, (5) The one of vigour. So he stood poised, (6) While he was on the upper horizon. (7) Then he drew near, and came down, (8) So as he was at a distance like that of two bows (joined together), rather even nearer. (9) Thus He (Allah) revealed to His slave what He revealed. (10) The heart did not err in what he saw. (11) Do you quarrel with him in what he sees? (12) Indeed he saw him another time (13) By Sidrat-ul-Muntaha (the lote-tree in the upper realm), (14) Near which there is Jannat-ul-Ma'wa (the Paradise of Abode), (15) When the lote-tree was covered by that which covered it. (16) The eye neither went wrong, nor did exceed the limit. (17) He has indeed seen a part of the biggest signs of your Lord. (18)

Think Critically

Allah could have told the Prophet about the five daily prayers while he was on Earth. Instead, he chose to tell him about them in the Heavens? Why?

Study  Questions

1 What is the name of the trip that Prophet Muhammad took on Al-Buraq? Where did he go first? After this stop, where did the Prophet go?

2 Who did the Prophet see in Jerusalem? What did he do there?

3 What did the Prophet see in the Heavens?

4 What did Allah order the Prophet to do before he went back to Earth?

5 What did the unbelievers say to Rasoolullah when he told them about his journey?

6 What did Abu Bakr do when he heard the story?

7 What name was Abu Bakr given after this incident? What does this name mean?

The Faithful Wife: Khadeejah Bintu Khuwayled

Questions?

1. Who was Khadeejah Bint Khuwayled?
2. Why did Prophet Muhammad run to her first when he needed help?
3. How did she respond to Prophet Muhammad?
4. Why do we call Khadeejah Umm-ul-Mu'mineen? What does that mean?

Main Idea: Khadeejah Bint Khuwayled was the first wife of Prophet Muhammad and the first woman to become a Muslim. She gave her husband, Rasoolullah, strong support. She is a good example to Muslims.

Word Watch

| Khadeejah Bint Khuwayled | خديجة بنت خُويلِد |
| Umm-ul-Mu'mineen | أُم المؤمنين |

The road seemed very long. Something strange happened in Ghar Hira. Rasoolullah ﷺ hurried home to tell Khadeejah about it. Something important had been revealed to him. He was breathing fast and his heart was pounding. What would he tell her? What would she think of him?

Khadeejah knew Rasoolullah ﷺ was always truthful and wise. She was with him all the time. But he worried that she might change her mind after this. He hoped that she would believe him, even though the story sounded strange.

Rasoolullah ﷺ finally got home. He was scared. He ran to his wife and said:

"Cover me. Cover me."
He told her about everything that had happened to him, and said, " I was scared; this has never happened to me before."

"Do not worry, Muhammad. I swear by Allah that He will never disappoint you," Khadeejah assured him. "You care about your family. You help the weak and the poor. You are hospitable to your guests, and you are always righteous." Khadeejah's words calmed him.

She had always stood by Rasoolullah's ﷺ side and supported him. She believed him with all her heart and soul. Khadeejah accepted Islam and became the first Muslim woman. She was an important early Muslim. She worked hard and spent her wealth for the sake of Allah.

Khadeejah is the first Umm-ul-Mu'mineen...the Mother of the Believers. We call each of the wives of Rasoolullah "Umm-ul-Mu'mineen."

Allah ﷻ sent Khadeejah رضي الله عنها greetings of peace with Rasoolullah ﷺ, informing her that she had a palace in Jannah. Allah also blessed both Khadeejah and Rasoolullah ﷺ with six children:

1. Al-Qasim
2. Abdullah
3. Zaynab
4. Ruqayyah
5. Um-Kulthoom
6. Fatimah

Rasoolullah ﷺ loved and admired Khadeejah very much. He once said:

"She (Khadeejah) had faith in me when people rejected me. She believed me when others refused, and supported me with her wealth when others denied me everything. And Allah, the Mighty and Glorious, gave me children by her, whereas He denied them to me with other women."

Rasoolullah ﷺ never married other women when Khadeejah was alive.

Great Lady Khadeejah

Great lady Khadeejah! Oh so wise, so fair, so good.
Great lady Khadeejah! Oh so wise, so good.

Khadeejah was a widow
No husband then had she.
She had to run her business without a family.

She heard of young Muhammad,
A merchant smart and true.
She sent for him and told him, "I'd like to hire you."

With fair and honest dealing
Khadeejah's business grew.
With thanks to young Muhammad, so honest and so true.

Though 15 years between them
Khadeejah thought it through.
She sent for him and told him, "I'd like to marry you."

They married then together
Began a family,
Lived many years together in love, quite happily.

In good times and in bad times,
She stayed right by his side.
She was the best example of a loving wife and bride.

Radiallahu Anha – May Allah be pleased with her!

Listen to this nasheed on Track 16 of your CD.

ACTIVITY time

Help Spread The Message: Khadeejah spent her wealth so that the message of Islam could reach more people. You can spread the message of Islam too. In groups of five or six, form a Da'wa committee. Your goal is to spread the message of Islam to other people. Brainstorm ideas and list ways of doing that. Use the paper on the following page to help in your project. Each group must pretend that the class is their audience, and they must use their ideas to spread the message of Islam to the class.

MY DA'WA COMMITTEE

The Name of my Committee is:
_____

The people in my Committee are:
_____
_____
_____
_____

The people we are going to spread the message of Islam to are:
_____

To spread the message of Islam, we are going to do the following:
_____
_____
_____
Marjia _____

Think Critically

Khadeejah supported Rasoolullah and helped him to teach people Islam. How can you help your elders to teach people the religion of Islam now?

Study Questions

1. How did Khadeejah رضي الله عنها treat Rasoolullah ﷺ before and after the revelation?

2. After becoming a Muslim, how did Khadeejah رضي الله عنها help our religion?

3. How can you tell that Rasoolullah ﷺ loved Khadeejah very much?

4. What can we learn from Khadeejah رضي الله عنها?

UNIT E

ISLAM IS CHARACTER

Did you know?

The dog's wet mouth is najis. So if a dog played with you and his saliva came on your body or clothes, you have to clean where he touched you very well with water.

HOW CAN YOU KEEP YOURSELF CLEAN?
HOW CAN MUSLIMS KEEP THEMSELVES AND THEIR SURROUNDINGS CLEAN?

Keep your body clean.

1. The Prophet ﷺ taught us the importance of taking regular baths. He especially reminded us to bathe before going to the Friday prayer, since it's our weekly holiday.

healthy habit

Try to take a bath every day

2. Keep your teeth clean.

Did you know that the angels dislike seeing a person praying while his teeth are dirty and have a bad smell? The Prophet ﷺ told us to clean our teeth and to keep them smelling fresh. He used "siwak" to brush his teeth. Today, we can use siwak or a toothbrush. Do you want to please Allah? Listen to this hadeeth:

The Prophet ﷺ said:

"Use siwak, for siwak cleans your mouth and pleases your Lord."

healthy habit

Brush your teeth with siwak or a tooth brush after each meal, or at least twice a day. Also make sure that your mouth is clean when you pray.

3. Keep your hair neat and your nails clipped.

When the Prophet ﷺ saw a man with messy hair, he nicely told him to comb his hair. The Prophet ﷺ also told us to keep our nails short and clean.

4. Observe Islamic etiquette when using the bathroom:

Islam taught us many ways to keep ourselves clean and pure. Let us list some of the manners when entering and leaving the toilet:

❶ Enter the bathroom with the left foot, and say the following du'aa':

"اللـهم إني أعوذ بك من الخُبثِ والخبـائث"

"Aallahumma inni a'oothu bikka min al-khubthi wal-khaba'ith"
"O Allah protect me from impurity and devils"

❷ When using the toilet, you should be alone where no one can see you.

❸ When you are finished using the bathroom, wash yourself with water.

❹ Before exiting the bathroom, wash your hands or make wudoo'.

❺ Do not play, talk, or spend extra time in the bathroom. When you are done using it, leave.

❻ Say "ghufranak غفرانك " which means "O Allah, I seek your forgiveness," and exit the bathroom starting with your right foot.

Keep your clothes clean and neat

Allah ﷻ said:

{ وَثِيَابَكَ فَطَهِّرْ }

"Wa thiyabak fatahhir"
And purify your clothes, (4)
Surah Al-Muddaththir 74: 4

Once the Prophet ﷺ saw a man wearing dirty clothes. He said, "Doesn't this man have anything to wash his clothes with?"

Think about it!

Amani was wearing a very expensive dress, but it was dirty.

Mona was wearing a simple dress that looked clean and neat.

Which do you think looked nicer? Why?

Bishay

Keep your surroundings clean

1. Keep your home clean

The Prophet ﷺ taught Muslims to keep their homes nice and clean. So when you see something that needs to be cleaned, go ahead and clean it. Keep your room clean. When you change your clothes, pick them up, and hang them where they belong. Don't throw them on the floor. Some of the ways to keep your home clean are:

1. Clean the table
2. Keep your room clean
3. Keep your clothes where they belong
4. Help wash the dishes
5. Take out the garbage
6. Help in vacuuming the house
7. Wipe off the dust
8. Ask your parents about more things you can do to help keep your home clean.

2. Keep your school clean

You should try to keep your school clean just like your house. Once a group of students at **Brighter Horizons Academy** took the job of cleaning the bathrooms. When they were asked, "Who told you to clean them?" they replied, "No one. We just like to keep our school clean."

3. Keep your Masjid clean

You should care for your masjid more than any other place: after all, a masjid is the House of Allah ﷻ. When you keep your masjid clean, you are greatly rewarded by Allah ﷻ.

HOW CAN I CLEAN THE MASJID?

1. Pick up litter
2. Take shoes off when you arrive
3. If something is spilled on the floor, get some paper towels and clean it up.
4. Do not eat inside the prayer hall.

Keep the Earth clean and green

Do not litter in the road, in the park, in the bus stop or in any public place. Always keep your city clean.

If you see litter in the park or on the road, just pick it up and put it in a trashcan. The Prophet ﷺ said:

"إماطة الأذى عن الطريق صدقة." رواه أحمد

"To remove litter or a harmful thing from the road is a charity."

Think Critically

How do cleanliness and taharah keep you healthy?

healthy

h a b i t

1. Try to keep wudoo', and be pure all the time.
2. Always smell good.
3. Always look clean and be clean inside out.

 Study  Questions

1 Why is it important to be clean all the time?

2 What is najasah, and how can you avoid it?

3 How can you keep your mouth healthy and clean?

4 How can you keep your home clean?

5 How can you keep your masjid clean?

6 How can you keep your school clean?

7 How can you keep the Earth clean?

Ta'awun...
Cooperation: It's My Strength!

Questions?

❶ Why is cooperation important?
❷ What are some ways that you cooperate?
❸ What teams are you a part of?

Main Idea: Working together as a team makes us stronger. If we are united, we can achieve great things. If we are divided, we will only do little things.

Word Watch

| Ta'awun (Cooperation) | تعاون |
| Unity | وِحدة |

Have you heard people talk about cooperation? Do you know what this big word means? Cooperation is a big word which means working together and helping each other. The Arabic word for cooperation is تعاون Ta'awun.

سورة المائدة

Surah Al-Maeda 5: 2

بِسْمِ ٱللَّهِ ٱلرَّحْمَٰنِ ٱلرَّحِيمِ

وَتَعَاوَنُوا۟ عَلَى ٱلْبِرِّ وَٱلتَّقْوَىٰ وَلَا تَعَاوَنُوا۟ عَلَى ٱلْإِثْمِ وَٱلْعُدْوَٰنِ وَٱتَّقُوا۟ ٱللَّهَ إِنَّ ٱللَّهَ شَدِيدُ ٱلْعِقَابِ ٢

TRANSLITERATION

"Wa ta'awanu ala albirri wa-ttaqwa wala ta'awanu al-al-ethmi wa-l'odwan wa-ttaqoo Allah Inna Allah shadeedu al'eqab"

MEANING TRANSLATION

... Help each other in righteousness and piety, and do not help each other in sin and aggression. Fear Allah. Surely, Allah is severe at punishment. (2)

Working together makes difficult tasks easier, and big jobs seem smaller. It makes the weak feel stronger, and it builds the community. Cooperation is a part of almost everything we do.

Ask yourself:

What would happen to you if you sat on a chair and one of its legs was missing? You would probably fall off the chair. The chair needs all of its legs to support your weight. Otherwise it cannot work properly.

MONA AND FATIMAH COOPERATE

Mona was a student in the third grade. She was smart and helpful towards others. Fatimah was a new girl in Mona's class. This was Fatimah's first year attending an Islamic school. She felt that the other kids knew more Qur'an, Arabic, and Islamic Studies than she. This made Fatimah very sad.

During recess, Fatimah sat alone. Mona came to Fatimah and asked if she would like to play with her and the other girls. With a big smile on her face, Fatimah went to play with them.

After school, during pick up time, Mona noticed that Fatimah had a sad face and tears in her eyes. She asked Fatimah why she was down. Fatimah told Mona that she felt sad because she could not catch up with the class in Qur'an and Arabic. Mona put her hand on Fatimah's shoulder and said, "You are new. It's okay not to know all the surahs as long as you try your best to learn." Mona offered to help Fatimah memorize Qur'an everyday after school while they waited for their parents to pick them up. Fatimah smiled and asked: "Really, you would do that for me?"

"Of course; you are my Muslim sister. What are friends for?" Mona answered.

A few weeks later, the class had a Qur'an test on Surat Al-A'la. Fatimah and Mona had been working together on it for days. When it was Fatimah's turn to recite, she completed the whole surah with only one small mistake. Their Qur'an teacher, Sister Amirah, was really impressed with Fatimah's improvement, and she asked her how she had done it. Fatimah answered, "I had a lot of help from Mona."

Sister Amirah was very pleased with Fatimah's answer. And she was very proud of Mona. She asked her to stand up and said, "When we cooperate, we are helping others and helping ourselves to become better people." Their teacher praised Mona for her kindness. "Class!" she said, "Fatimah and Mona have just shown us what we can accomplish if we work together to do something good! Allahu Akbar."

Mona's classmates gave a loud takbeer for her cooperation!

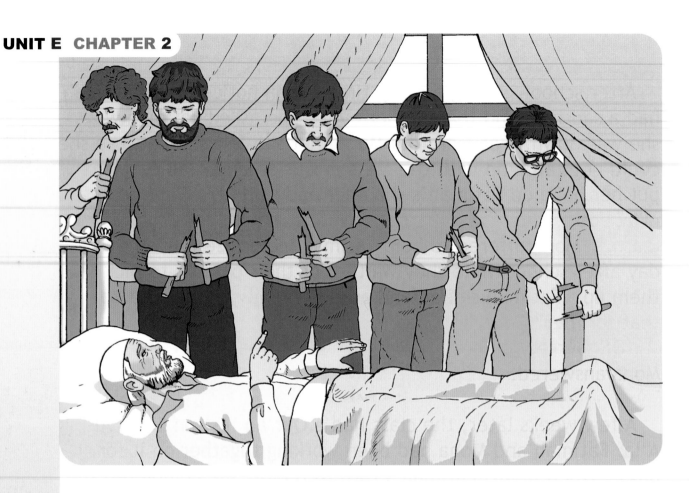

Story Time
THE DYING MAN

Once upon a time there was an old Muslim man who was very sick. The man wanted to teach his children an important lesson before he died. He asked one of them to bring him a bunch of twigs.

The father took the bunch apart and gave one twig to each of his sons. He asked each one of them to break one twig. They all broke the twigs very easily.

Then the father tied the rest of the twigs back together and gave the whole bunch to his strongest son. He asked him to break the bunch. The strong son tried and tried but could not break the twigs. Together, the bunch was too strong to break.

The father looked at his children and said:

"My children, always stay together because you are just like this bunch of twigs: united you stand; divided you fall."

Have you heard what the Prophet said about cooperation?

WORDS OF WISDOM
(Hadeeth Shareef)

حديث شريف

Narrated By Bukhari & Muslim

عن أَبِي مُوسَى الأشعري رضي الله عنه: قال رسول الله ﷺ :

"الْمُؤْمِنُ لِلْمُؤْمِنِ كَالْبُنْيَانِ يَشُدُّ بَعْضُهُ بَعْضًا ثُمَّ شَبَّكَ بَيْنَ أَصَابِعِهِ" رواه البخاري ومسلم

TRANSLITERATION

"Al-mu'minu lil-mu'mini kal-bonyan yashuddu ba'dahu ba'dan, thumma shabbaka bayna asabi'ahu."

MEANING TRANSLATION

While the Prophet ﷺ was saying this hadeeth, he clasped his hands together, and put his fingers together:

"A believer to a believer is like a strong building; each part supports the other".

This hadeeth shows us the importance of unity. Unity means "sticking together," or working together as one team. Here are some stories about unity.

Everyone Does His Part!

Prophet Muhammad ﷺ was once traveling with a group of Sahabah. They stopped at a place to eat and rest. They decided to slaughter a sheep and roast it.

"I will do the slaughtering," said one of them.
"I will remove the skin," said the other.
The third one said, "I will do the roasting."

Each one of them volunteered to do one piece of work. Rasoolullah said, "I will collect the firewood."

The companions said, "O Rasoolullah! Don't bother yourself. We will do everything."

The Prophet ﷺ said, "I know you can do everything. But I do not like to sit while you are working. I do not want to be a person who distinguishes himself from his companions."
The Prophet ﷺ went and brought firewood.

Think Critically:

❶ In what ways is a strong brick building like a group of cooperating Muslims? Mention three ways.

❷ What would prevent a Muslim child from cooperating with his brothers and sisters in Islam?

Think about it!

How do you support your friends?
How do your friends support you?
How do you feel if you do not have anyone to help you?
How do you think Fatimah felt when Mona offered to help her?

Study  Questions

❶ What is the Arabic word for cooperation?

❷ Why did Mona want to help Fatimah?

❸ How did Mona's help change Fatimah's life?

❹ What did the old dying man teach his five sons?

❺ Recite an ayah about cooperation.

❻ Recite a hadeeth about cooperation.

Ta'awun: Cooperation in My Daily Life

Questions?

❶ Can we be happy in life without cooperation?
❷ Can we be successful in our life without cooperation?
❸ Do you feel happier when your whole family wins something together, or when you win something alone?

Main Idea: To be happy and successful, you have to know your role in the team. And you should accomplish what you are expected to do.

Word Watch

Ta'awun   تعاون
(Cooperation)

Ta'awun, or cooperation, is an important pillar of success in our daily life. Allah loves those who cooperate with each other. The Prophet taught us how doing things in jama'ah is always better. He taught us to pray in jama'ah behind an imam, and to travel in jama'ah with an ameer, or a leader. Jama'ah is the Arabic word for a group or a team.

THE THREE FRIENDS

Once upon a time there were three friends: a fisherman, a tailor, and a merchant. All three were looking for work, but none had been successful.

One day, they decided to leave town and look for work somewhere else. On their journey, they met a wise man. The friends told their story to the wise man and asked him for advice. He looked at them and said, "Why don't you work together, instead of working separately?" The three friends liked his advice and decided to follow it.
The tailor said, "I will make clothes."
The merchant said, "I will sell the clothes."
The fisherman said, "I will take the clothes in my boat to be sold in the towns around here."

They worked as a team. That way they each had a job and they all succeeded.

Playing on a Team

The men in the story worked as a team. Are you a part of any teams? You may be on a sports team, like a soccer or basketball team, but even if you are not, everyone is part of many teams in their life.

Your family is a very important team that works together so that things will run smoothly at home. Your class and community also work together like a team; each one of us has an important role to play in each of the teams in our lives. Sometimes you may be the star player on the team. Other times you might play a small supporting role. But in every case, the part that you play matters.

In order for any team to perform at its best, every member of the team must cooperate with the others and do his or her best! Remember,

YOUR JOB IS IMPORTANT...YOU ARE PART OF A TEAM!!

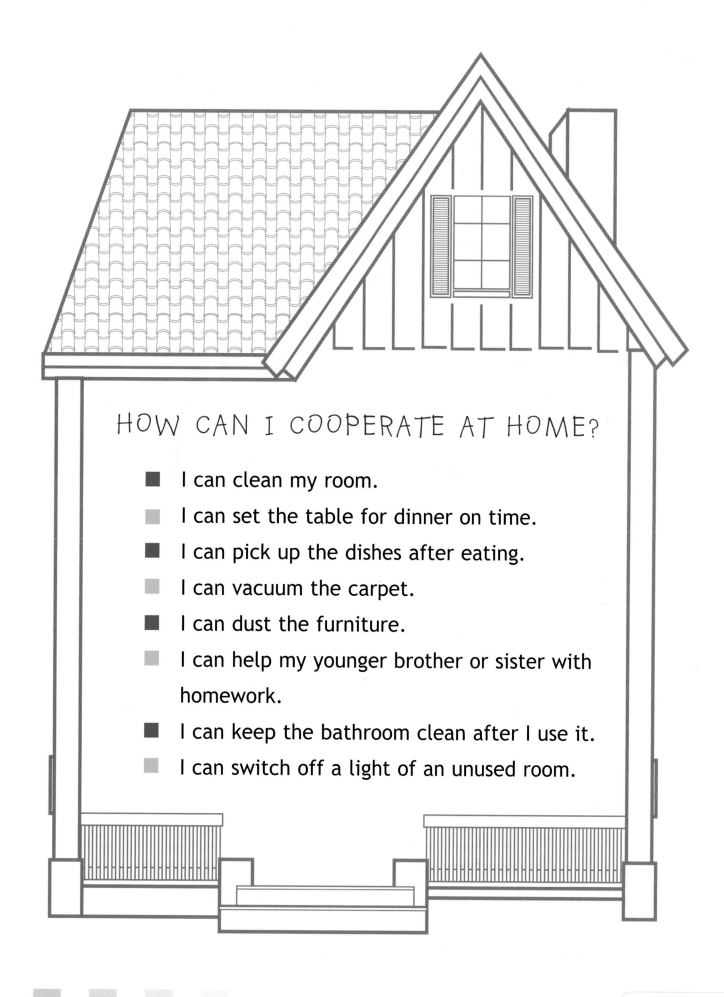

HOW CAN I COOPERATE AT HOME?

- I can clean my room.
- I can set the table for dinner on time.
- I can pick up the dishes after eating.
- I can vacuum the carpet.
- I can dust the furniture.
- I can help my younger brother or sister with homework.
- I can keep the bathroom clean after I use it.
- I can switch off a light of an unused room.

HOW CAN I PRACTICE TA'AWUN AT SCHOOL?

- I can keep my desk clean.
- I can clean under my desk.
- I can pick up litter.
- I can hold the door for my teacher.
- I can clean the tables after lunch.
- I can help my friends carry their books.
- I can recite the du'aa' and Qur'an (Athkar) during morning assembly together with my peers.

HOW CAN I PRACTCE TA'AWUN AT THE MASJID?

- I can help keep the masjid clean.
- I can keep my voice low.
- I can walk slowly and follow the rules of the masjid.
- I can give charity.
- I can stand in a straight line during salah, shoulder to shoulder with my neighbor, without looking around, and without talking.
- I can encourage my friends to come to the masjid.
- I can teach others about the manners we should have in the masjid.

E25

EXAMPLE OF COOPERATION AT THE KHAN FAMILY:

The Khan Family has a chore chart; this helps each member of the family to know his or her job. This helps their team to cooperate and run their home smoothly.

Doing the dishes	Zaynab and Asim
Cleaning the backyard	Dad and Aqeel
Vacuuming the carpet	Farah
Grocery shopping	Dad and Farah
Folding the laundry	Zaynab and Farah
Helping with dinner	Mom, Asim, and Zaynab
Praying on time	Everyone
Going to the masjid	Together

healthy

h a b i t

Always offer to help someone who needs help. Do not wait for them to ask you. This is part of cooperation!

We Have Learned:

1. When we work as a team we can accomplish great things

2. When we help others we are pleasing Allah.

3. When we work together we become stronger.

4. United we stand, divided we fall.

5. Allah helps us through one another.

6. Cooperation is a way to earn hasanat.

When we cooperate we are working like the hand. Our fingers are different, but they all belong to one hand, and they're all important.

ACTIVITY time

Tonight sit down with your family and make a chart like the Khan family. Try to follow this chart for a whole week. Write a paragraph about this experience. Did your home run more smoothly when everyone knew their job?

WORDS OF WISDOM
Holy Qur'an

سورة آل عمران

Al-E-Imran 3: 103

بِسْمِ اللَّهِ الرَّحْمَٰنِ الرَّحِيمِ

وَاعْتَصِمُوا بِحَبْلِ اللَّهِ جَمِيعًا وَلَا تَفَرَّقُوا ۚ وَاذْكُرُوا نِعْمَتَ اللَّهِ عَلَيْكُمْ إِذْ كُنتُمْ أَعْدَاءً فَأَلَّفَ بَيْنَ قُلُوبِكُمْ فَأَصْبَحْتُم بِنِعْمَتِهِ إِخْوَانًا وَكُنتُمْ عَلَىٰ شَفَا حُفْرَةٍ مِّنَ النَّارِ فَأَنقَذَكُم مِّنْهَا ۗ كَذَٰلِكَ يُبَيِّنُ اللَّهُ لَكُمْ آيَاتِهِ لَعَلَّكُمْ تَهْتَدُونَ ۝

TRANSLITERATION

Wa'tasimoo bihabli-llahi jamee'an wala tafarraqoo wathkuroo ni'mat-Allahi alaykum ith kuntum a'da'an fa'allafa bayna quloobikum faasbahtum bini'matihi ikhwanan wakuntum ala shafa hufratin mina nnari faanqathakum minha kathalika yubayyinu-llahu lakum ayatihi la'allakum tahtadoon

MEANING TRANSLATION

Hold fast, all of you, to the cord of Allah, and be not divided. Remember the blessing of Allah upon you: When you were enemies to each other, and He brought your hearts together, so that, you became brothers through His blessing. You were at the brink of a pit of Fire, then He saved you from it. This is how Allah makes His signs clear to you, so that you may take the right path. (103)

Think Critically

1 How does Salatul Jama'ah teach us cooperation and team work?

2 What are the teams you are a part of?

3 What is your role on each of these teams?

4 Make a chart illustrating your role on each of these teams. Are you a star player or a supporting player on these teams?

5 What is more important to you: to be famous, or to help your team win?

Study  Questions

1 Why did the tailor, the merchant, and the boatman follow the wise man's advice?

2 Could they have worked separately?

3 Did they make a good decision to work together? Why or why not?

4 What is the Arabic word for group or team?

Perseverance: It's my challenge!
WORK HARD & DON'T GIVE UP

Questions?

1. Was it easy for Prophet Muhammad ﷺ to spread the message of Islam?
2. Did he give up?
3. Do you work hard to achieve your goals?
4. If something is hard to do, should we give up?

Main Idea: Sometimes in life we will face challenges. A Muslim asks Allah for help, works hard, and does not give up.

Word Watch

Thabat (Perseverance)	ثبات
Goal	هدف

Who is an Achiever?

An **achiever** is someone who works hard and keeps doing that until he reaches his or her **goal**. An achiever is someone who perseveres. **Perseverance** is a big word for "not giving up." **Thabat** is the Arabic word for perseverance.

Now! Are you an achiever?

THE PROPHET ﷺ IS THE BEST EXAMPLE OF PERSEVERENCE, "Thabat."

Our beloved Prophet Muhammad ﷺ taught us the value of hard work and perseverance. When he was ordered by Allah ﷻ to teach Islam, many people did not accept him. They made fun of him. They even tried to kill him. One time they offered to give him a lot of money and make him the king of Makkah if he quit teaching Islam. But he refused to give up. Prophet Muhammad ﷺ was an achiever. He told his enemies that no matter how much they gave him, he would never give up his mission.

The non-believers also hurt his friends. Among those who got hurt were the family of Yasir. The kuffar tortured and hurt them, but they never gave up. For their perseverance and thabat, they were promised Paradise by the Prophet ﷺ. They too were great achievers.

A friend of the Prophet ﷺ named Bilal Ibn Rabah was left in the heat of the desert with a huge rock on his chest. The kuffar wanted him to leave Islam, but Bilal did not give up. Bilal was also an achiever.

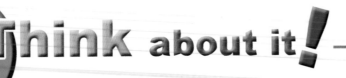

Think about it!

What would have happened if Prophet Muhammad had given up?

What would have happened if the Sahabah had given up?

Here are some stories about kids like you:

DON'T GIVE UP

The teacher was passing back the test papers back. When Zaid received his paper, he did not like what he saw: his test grade was very low. Zaid frowned. He felt sad. The teacher said, "It is your choice, Zaid. You can keep this grade, or you can take a make-up test. And remember, a Muslim should never give up and should always work hard like our Prophet Muhammad ﷺ ."

Zaid thought about what his teacher said. When he got home, he chose to study hard. He was determined to get a good grade. When Zaid took his test this time, he got an "A." Zaid showed perseverance and won the prize for hard work, a big "A," and a hug from Mom and Dad.

YES, I CAN

Bilal was so excited. His father came home with a new skateboard for him. He thanked his father. "Can you teach me how to ride it, Dad?" said Bilal.

"Of course," said his dad. "We will start this weekend."

Bilal had a tough time learning how to ride his skateboard. Every time he rode it, he fell. Bilal quit the lesson and sat under a pear tree in his backyard. While he was sitting, he noticed an ant climbing up the tree. Every time it tried to climb, it fell off. It tried five times, and each time it fell it climbed right back up. On the sixth time, the ant climbed the tree and made it all the way up without falling.

TAKBIR!

Bilal learned a big lesson from the tiny ant. He learned that sometimes one can fail, but one cannot give up. Bilal went to his father and asked him to teach him how to ride the skateboard the next day. Bilal was not a quitter. Bilal did not give up.

You do not fail if you fall down. You fail if you stay down.

We have learned:

1. Most of the time, you need to work hard to achieve your goals.

2. Whenever we fail, we should try again. This is perseverance.

3. The best example of a hard worker is Prophet Muhammad.

4. Do your best, and never be a quitter.

5. Do not give up! Say "Insha'Allah I will try my best."

 time

Write a paragraph about a time when you did not give up. Tell the class what you learned and how you benefited from this experience.

DO YOU WANT TO BE THE BEST?

WORK HARD,

BECAUSE THE BEST NEVER REST!

WORDS OF WISDOM
Holy Qur'an

سورة البروج
Surah Al-Burooj 85: 1-22

بِسْمِ ٱللَّهِ ٱلرَّحْمَٰنِ ٱلرَّحِيمِ

وَٱلسَّمَآءِ ذَاتِ ٱلْبُرُوجِ ﴿١﴾ وَٱلْيَوْمِ ٱلْمَوْعُودِ ﴿٢﴾ وَشَاهِدٍ وَمَشْهُودٍ ﴿٣﴾ قُتِلَ أَصْحَٰبُ ٱلْأُخْدُودِ ﴿٤﴾ ٱلنَّارِ ذَاتِ ٱلْوَقُودِ ﴿٥﴾ إِذْ هُمْ عَلَيْهَا قُعُودٌ ﴿٦﴾ وَهُمْ عَلَىٰ مَا يَفْعَلُونَ بِٱلْمُؤْمِنِينَ شُهُودٌ ﴿٧﴾ وَمَا نَقَمُوا۟ مِنْهُمْ إِلَّآ أَن يُؤْمِنُوا۟ بِٱللَّهِ ٱلْعَزِيزِ ٱلْحَمِيدِ ﴿٨﴾ ٱلَّذِى لَهُۥ مُلْكُ ٱلسَّمَٰوَٰتِ وَٱلْأَرْضِ وَٱللَّهُ عَلَىٰ كُلِّ شَىْءٍ شَهِيدٌ ﴿٩﴾ إِنَّ ٱلَّذِينَ فَتَنُوا۟ ٱلْمُؤْمِنِينَ وَٱلْمُؤْمِنَٰتِ ثُمَّ لَمْ يَتُوبُوا۟ فَلَهُمْ عَذَابُ جَهَنَّمَ وَلَهُمْ عَذَابُ ٱلْحَرِيقِ ﴿١٠﴾ إِنَّ ٱلَّذِينَ ءَامَنُوا۟ وَعَمِلُوا۟ ٱلصَّٰلِحَٰتِ لَهُمْ جَنَّٰتٌ تَجْرِى مِن تَحْتِهَا ٱلْأَنْهَٰرُ ذَٰلِكَ ٱلْفَوْزُ ٱلْكَبِيرُ ﴿١١﴾ إِنَّ بَطْشَ رَبِّكَ لَشَدِيدٌ ﴿١٢﴾ إِنَّهُۥ هُوَ يُبْدِئُ وَيُعِيدُ ﴿١٣﴾ وَهُوَ ٱلْغَفُورُ ٱلْوَدُودُ ﴿١٤﴾ ذُو ٱلْعَرْشِ ٱلْمَجِيدُ ﴿١٥﴾ فَعَّالٌ لِّمَا يُرِيدُ ﴿١٦﴾ هَلْ أَتَىٰكَ حَدِيثُ ٱلْجُنُودِ ﴿١٧﴾ فِرْعَوْنَ وَثَمُودَ ﴿١٨﴾ بَلِ ٱلَّذِينَ كَفَرُوا۟ فِى تَكْذِيبٍ ﴿١٩﴾ وَٱللَّهُ مِن وَرَآئِهِم مُّحِيطٌ ﴿٢٠﴾ بَلْ هُوَ قُرْءَانٌ مَّجِيدٌ ﴿٢١﴾ فِى لَوْحٍ مَّحْفُوظٍ ﴿٢٢﴾

Bismi-llahi-rrahmani-rraheem

(1) Wassama'i thati-lburooj

(2) Walyawmi-lmaw'ood

(3) Washahidiw-wamash-hood

(4) Qutila as-habu-lukhdoodi

(5) Annari thati-lwaqood

(6) Ith hum alayha qu'ood

(7) Wahum ala ma yafaloona bilmu'mineena shuhood

(8) Wama naqamoo minhum illa ay-yu'minoo billahi alazeezi-lhameedi

(9) Allathee lahu mulku-ssamawati wal-ardi wallahu ala kulli shay'in shaheed

(10) Inna-llatheena fatanoo-lmu'mineena walmuminati thumma lam yatooboo falahum athabu jahannama walahum athabu-lhareeq

(11) Inna allatheena amanoo wa'amiloo ssalihati lahum jannatun tajree min tahtihal-anharu thalika-lfawzu-lkabeer

(12) Inna batsha rabbika lashadeed

(13) Innahu huwa yubdi'o wayueed

(14) Wahuwa-lghafooru alwadood

(15) Thu arshi-lmajeed

(16) Fa'alul-lima yureed

(17) Hal ataka hadeethu-ljunoodi

(18) Fir'awna wa thamood

(19) Bali-llatheena kafaroo fee taktheeb

(20) Wallahu miw wara'ihim muheet

(21) Bal huwa qur'anum-majeed

(22) Fee lawhim-mahfooth

I swear by the sky, the one having stellar formations, (1) And by the Promised Day, (2) And by that which attends, and that which is attended, (3) Cursed were the People of the Trench, (4) The (people of the) fire that was rich with fuel, (5) When they were sitting by it, (6) And were watching what they were doing with the believers. (7) They punished them for nothing but that they believed in Allah, the All-Mighty, the Worthy of All Praise, (8) The One to whom belongs the Kingdom of the heavens and the earth. And Allah is witness over every thing. (9) Surely, those who persecuted the believing men and the believing women, then did not repent, _for them there is the torment of Jahannam (Hell), and for them there is the torment of burning. (10) As for those who believed and did righteous deeds, for them there are gardens beneath which rivers flow. That is the big achievement. (11) The seizure of your Lord is severe indeed! (12) Surely He originates (creation) and repeats (it after death). (13) And He is the Most-Forgiving, the Most-Loving, (14) The Master of the Throne, the Glorious. (15) He is ever doer of what He intends. (16) Has there come to you the story of the forces, (17) Of Fir'aun (Pharaoh) and Thamud? (18) But those who disbelieve are (engaged) in denying (the truth). (19) Allah has encompassed them from all sides. (20) The reality is that it is the glorious Qur'an, (21) Recorded) in the Preserved Tablet (Lauh Mahfuz). (22)

Think Critically

If your goal is good, you should work hard to achieve it. What if you discover that what you are trying to do is NOT good?

Study  Questions

1. What is the Arabic word for perseverance?

2. How do you think Zaid felt when he did poorly on the test?

3. What would you have done if you were in Zaid's place?

4. How do you think Zaid felt when he got an "A" on his make-up test?

5. What would have happened if Zaid had given up?

6. What did Bilal do when he fell off the skateboard? Why?

7. What did Bilal learn from the ant?

RESPECT: It's My Duty!

Questions?

1 What does respect mean?
2 Whom should we respect? Why?
3 Do you like to be respected?
4 What are some ways we can show respect?

Main Idea: Allah ordered us to respect others, and the Prophet taught us how to do that.
In life, if we respect others, we will be respected.

Word Watch

Respect   احترام

Allah سبحانه وتعالى sent prophets to show us how to worship Him and how to treat each other. Prophet Muhammad ﷺ told us that he was sent to perfect our manners. One of the most important manners of a Muslim is respect.

WHAT DOES RESPECT MEAN?

Respect means showing someone that they are important, and that you care about what they say and do. When you care about someone's feelings, you respect them. Islam pays special attention to respecting parents and elders. We should always treat children with kindness, and elders with respect.

Here is what the Prophet ﷺ taught us about respect:

WORDS OF WISDOM

(Hadeeth Shareef)

حديث شريف

Narrated By Abu Dawood

عَنْ أَبِي هُرَيْرَةَ رضي الله عنه: قَالَ رَسُولُ اللَّهِ ﷺ :
"خَيْرُكُمْ إِسْلَامًا أَحَاسِنُكُمْ أَخْلَاقًا إِذَا فَقُهُوا"

رواه أبو داود

TRANSLITERATION

"Khayrukum Islaman ahasinukum akhlaqan ith faquhoo"

MEANING TRANSLATION

Abu Hurayrah reported that Rasoolullah ﷺ said:
"The best of you in Islam are those who have the best manners and learned the religion well."

When the Prophet's friends talked to him, they lowered their voices, and they did not shout in his presence. The Prophet's friends were showing respect. One time, Abu Bakr and Omar argued in front of Rasoolullah, and they raised their voices over his voice. Allah then revealed some ayat ordering Muslims not to raise their voices over the Prophet's voice. When Abu Bakr and Omar heard the order of Allah, they apologized and never raised their voices again. We should respect our parents, teachers, and elders. One way to respect them is not to raise our voices over theirs.

Respect in our lives...

For our Parents

Once Ahmad did something wrong. So his father scolded him, but he did not answer back. He knew he was wrong. He apologized to his father. Ahmad showed respect.

Zaynab was walking home with her parents. When they got home, Zaynab held the door open and let her parents enter first. Zaynab showed respect.

Iman asked her mother for a cool new toy that she had seen at the store. Her mother said, "No, Iman. I'm afraid you have enough toys. Maybe you will get it for Eid, inshaAllah." Iman was disappointed, but she smiled politely and said: "Okay, InshaAllah." Iman obeyed her mother and did not argue. She showed respect.

For our Elders

Zaid and Leena visited their grandparents. When they saw them, they kissed their hands and gave them a big hug. Zaid and Leena showed respect.

Fadi was sitting with his family when his aunt Basimah came. There was no empty chair in the room. Fadi offered his seat to his aunt. She thanked him for that. Fadi was showing respect.

When someone is speaking

Yousef sat down during Jumu'a with his father, listening to the imam. Yousef did not talk during the entire khutba. Yousef was showing respect.

Ameer needed help with his homework. He went to ask his father, but he was on the telephone. He waited for him to finish before he asked him his question. By not interrupting him, Ameer showed respect.

Respecting Teachers and the Principal

Jamilah knew the answer to her teacher's question, but the teacher was not finished speaking. Jamilah raised her hand and waited patiently to be called on before she spoke. By not calling out the answer, Jamilah showed respect.

At school, the principal saw a boy who was wasting a lot of water while making wudoo'. The principal was not pleased with the boy because he was not using water properly. The boy apologized to the principal and nodded his head, showing respect.

For the Feelings of Others

Amal and Samia were talking to each other in Arabic. Zainab came to join them, but she could not speak Arabic. Amal and Samia started speaking English so that Zainab could understand them. They showed respect for her feelings.

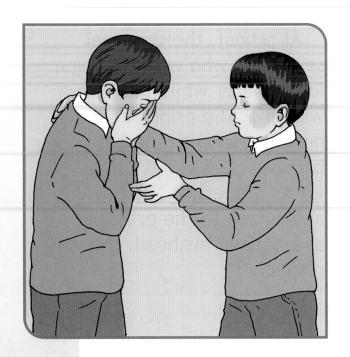

Rami did poorly on a test. He told Khalid. Khalid did not make fun of Rami. He encouraged Rami and told him that he would do better next time insha Allah. Khalid showed respect.

For the Privacy of Others

The Prophet ﷺ told us that when visiting someone, we should knock three times. If no one answers, even if we think they are home, we should leave quietly. By doing that, we show respect.

Saad saw the mail sitting on the kitchen table. There was a big package that looked very interesting, but it had his mother's name on it. Saad left the package on the table and did not open it. He showed respect.

Neha heard her sister and her friend laughing in the room. When she knocked on the door, her sister told her not to come in. Neha was annoyed, but she did not stand by the door and listen. She went to her own room. Neha showed respect.

For the Property of Others

Hamzah and Layth were playing with Hamzah's soccer ball. Layth kicked the ball into a mud puddle by mistake. He apologized and helped Hamzah clean up the ball. Layth showed respect.

Dina borrowed Lamya's book. She kept it clean and safe in her drawer so that her younger sister would not tear its pages. She returned Lamya's book as good as new. Dina showed respect.

YOU HAVE A DUTY
TO RESPECT OTHERS

AND THE RIGHT
TO BE RESPECTED

What did we learn from this?

1. We should respect all people.

2. When you respect others, others will respect you.

3. Allah ﷻ loves those who show respect.

4. When showing respect, we are following Prophet Muhammad ﷺ.

5. Respecting our elders is one of the most important types of respect.

6. Respect has many parts. We show respect for people's feelings, privacy, and property.

MY TOWER OF RESPECT

I respect Allah by obeying Him

I respect My Prophet by following his teachings

I respect my parents by listening to them

I respect my teachers by doing my work and following the rules

I show respect to myself by obeying Allah, serving my Muslim community and being kind to others. If I do this Allah will be pleased with me. Ths is the best respect I would give to myself

We should also respect the privacy of others and their property. This means that if something does not belong to us we should not open it or look through it. And if two people are talking, we should not spy on them or try to find out what they are saying. It also means that we should take care of things, even if they do not belong to us. These are all parts of respect.

Think Critically:

1. Respecting others makes your life happy and easy. Disrespecting them causes you many troubles and problems. Explain how.

Study Questions

1 What is respect?

2 Recite a hadeeth about respecting elders.

3 Mention three things you do to show respect to your parents.

4 Mention three things you do to show respect to your teachers.

5 Mention three things you do to show respect to your elders.

6 How do you respect the privacy of others?

7 How do you respect the property of others?

TRUTHFULNESS: الصّـدق
IT'S MY STYLE!

Questions?

1. Why is it important to tell the truth?
2. What happens if someone does not tell the truth?
3. Is telling the truth always easy?
4. Is it alright to lie when you are joking or if you are in trouble?

Main Idea: A Muslim must be truthful in everything he says and does. The prophet was truthful and honest.

Word Watch

As-Sidq الصّـدق
Sadiq صادِقْ

How would you feel if someone promised you a gift, and then never gave it to you? Would you still trust him or her? How about if your friend told you that she had a great new toy, and then you found out that she was lying? Would you believe her the next time she told you something?

The Prophet ﷺ taught us to be truthful in our words and actions, even when we are joking. Once upon a time, the Prophet ﷺ was sitting with Abdullah bin Amer. Abdullah's mother called him and said, "Come Abdullah. I want to give you something." The Prophet asked her, "What are you going to give him?" She said, "I want to give him some dates." The Prophet said, "If you had not given him anything, it would have been written against you as a lie."

HOW CAN I OWN A HOUSE IN JANNAH?

عَنْ أَبِي أُمَامَةَ رضي الله عنه : قَالَ رَسُولُ اللَّهِ ﷺ :

"أَنَا زَعِيمٌ بِبَيْتٍ فِي وَسَطِ الْجَنَّةِ لِمَنْ تَرَكَ الْكَذِبَ وَإِنْ كَانَ مَازِحًا" رواه أبو داود

The Prophet ﷺ promised truthful Muslims a house in the middle of Jannah.

Allah (is) Al-Haqq

الـحـق

THE TRUTH

Allah always tells us the truth and wants us to always speak the truth.

Allah says: " الله يهدي للحق Allah guides to the truth." (10:35)

The Lying Shepherd

HELP ME!

Once upon a time, there was a boy named Kareem. Kareem's father taught him how to take care of sheep. Kareem became a very good shepherd.

Kareem's father warned him to watch out for wolves because they might eat the sheep.

One day Kareem got bored while watching the herd. He decided to play a trick (a joke) on the people of the village. Kareem yelled, "Help! Help! The wolf is coming for the herd." People rushed to help him. To their surprise, there was no wolf, and the sheep were fine.

Kareem's joke was not funny. The people did not like what he did. But he laughed at the surprise on their faces, and he thought that what he had done was really clever and funny.

The next day, Kareem got bored again, and again he played the same cruel joke. He yelled, "Wolf! Wolf! Help us!" The people of the village rushed to help him. Again, they found out that there was no wolf.

The people of the village were angry and decided that Kareem could not be trusted.

Early the next day, Kareem was watching the sheep again, and a real scary wolf came. Kareem started screaming and yelling for help. The people ignored Kareem's cries. They thought he was playing another joke like before. The wolf attacked the herd and ate one of his father's sheep. Because of Kareem's lies, no one helped him, and he paid for his big mistake.

I WILL ALWAYS TELL THE TRUTH

You may have heard this story before; it is a very well known tale. The star of the story, Kareem, learned a hard lesson about lying and the value of truthfulness. When a person keeps lying, people stop trusting him. Worst of all, he gets bad deeds (sayyi'at).

Kareem asked Allah to forgive him. He apologized to the people of the village, and they forgave him. From that day on, Kareem tried to always be truthful.

A SPOT ON THE SOUL

Every time a person tells a lie, a black spot is put on his soul. When his whole soul is covered with dark spots, he becomes known to Allah ﷻ as a liar. But how can you get rid of the dark spots on your soul? By telling the truth.

Once, Abdu-Rahman had his friend Zaid over at his house. They were in the kitchen having a snack. Abdur-Rahman went into the cupboard to get two glasses so he and his friend could have juice. When Abdur-Rahman reached into the shelf, a few of his mom's glasses fell to the floor and broke. Abdur-Rahman was worried. What was he going to tell his mother? "Tell your mom the truth," said Zaid. "If you don't, things will become much worse." Abdur-Rahman looked at Zaid and said, "What do you mean?" Zaid continued:

"First, you'll be telling a lie.

Second, you'll get a black spot on your soul.

Third, and most importantly, you'll be disobeying Allah and His Prophet ﷺ ."

Abdur-Rahman replied, "You are right. I will tell the truth insha Allah."

Abdur-Rahman went to his mother and told her what had happened. The first thing his mother asked was if he was alright, then she told him to be more careful next time. Abdur-Rahman hugged his mother. He felt relieved that she was not angry, and that she was proud of him for telling the truth. Abdur-Rahman's mom put her arms around him and said, "Son, remember what the Prophet ﷺ said: 'الصِّدقُ طُمَأنينة Truthfulness is peace of mind.'"

Abdur-Rahman thanked his friend Zaid for helping him make the right choice by telling the truth.

THE PROPHET HATED LYING

A'isha, the wife of Prophet Muhammad ﷺ said:
"The most hated behavior to the Prophet ﷺ was lying."

Who was known as the Truthful and the Trustworthy الصادق الأمين ?
It is Prophet Muhammad ﷺ

WORDS OF WISDOM
Hadeeth Shareef

حديث شريف

Narrated By Ahmed

عَنْ عَبْدِ اللَّهِ بن مسعود رضي الله عنه: قَالَ رَسُولُ اللَّهِ ﷺ :

"عَلَيْكُمْ بِالصِّدْقِ فَإِنَّ الصِّدْقَ يَهْدِي إِلَى الْبِرِّ وَإِنَّ الْبِرَّ يَهْدِي إِلَى الْجَنَّةِ وَإِنَّهُ الرَّجُلَ لَيَصْدُقُ وَيَتَحَرَّى الصِّدْقَ حَتَّى يُكْتَبَ عِنْدَ اللَّهِ صِدِّيقًا وَإِيَّاكُمْ وَالْكَذِبَ فَإِنَّ الْكَذِبَ يَهْدِي إِلَى الْفُجُورِ وَالْفُجُورَ يَهْدِي إِلَى النَّارِ وَإِنَّ الرَّجُلَ لَيَكْذِبُ حَتَّى يُكْتَبَ عِنْدَ اللَّهِ كَذَّابًا"

TRANSLITERATION

Alaykum bis-Sidq, fa innas-Sidqa yahdi ilal-birr, wa innal-birra yahdi ilal-Jannah. Wa inna-arrajula laysduqa hatta yuktaba ind Allahi siddeeqa. Wa iyyakum wal kathib, fa innal kathiba yahdi ilal-fujoor, wa innal fujoora yahdi ilan-narr. Wa inna-arrajula layakthiba hatta yuktaba inda Allahi kathaba.

MEANING TRANSLATION

Abdullah Ibn Mas'ood reported that Prophet Muhammad ﷺ said: "Be truthful, for truthfulness leads to goodness, and goodness leads to Jannah. And a man would keep telling the truth untill Allah writes his name as a truthful person. Beware of lying, for lying leads to wrong-doing, and wrong-doing leads to hellfire. And a man would keep lying until Allah writes his name as a liar."

What did we learn from this?

❶ Telling the truth brings you closer to Allah.

❷ Telling the truth earns you the trust of others.

❸ Telling the truth gives you peace of mind.

❹ Telling the truth leads you to Jannah.

❺ Our role model in being truthful is Prophet Muhammad ﷺ .

❻ Prophet Muhammad ﷺ promised a house in Jannah for those who do not lie.

❼ When a person lies then asks for Allah's forgiveness, Allah ﷻ forgives him.

❽ Telling the truth may seem hard, but lying will get you in much more trouble.

❾ Make sure you think before you speak.
Ask yourself: "Will my words be the truth, or not?"

Before you speak, think of the following:

Stop and think.

Is it truthful? Is it right?

Go ahead and speak the truth!

Think Critically:

1 Truthfulness leads to peace of mind. How?

2 Lying leads to big trouble. Why?

Study Questions

1 Was Rasoolullah a truthful person? Did people trust him?

2 Why is it difficult for some people to tell the truth?

3 What is the reward for people who tell the truth?

4 What is the reward for people who tell the truth, even when they are kidding or telling jokes?

5 What is the punishment for liars?

6 What lessons did you learn from the story of the lying shepherd?

7 Was Abdur-Rahman in trouble when he told his mother the truth about the broken cups? Why?

8 Write a hadeeth about the importance of telling the truth and the danger of telling lies?

Saying It the Prophet's Way

Questions?

1. Would you like to be with the Prophet in Jannah?
2. Do you like to do things like the Prophet used to do?
3. What should Muslims say when they greet each other?
4. How do you feel when someone says "Assalamu alaykum" or "jazak Allahu khayran" to you?
5. Do you use Islamic words when you talk to people?

Main Idea: To learn the proper Islamic expressions that we should use in our everyday lives.

Word Watch

Assalamu alaykum	السلام عليكم
Bismillahi-rrahmani-rraheem	بسم الله الرحمن الرَّحيم
Jazakum-ullah Khayran	جزاكم الله خيرا
Wa Iyyakum Insha-Allah	وإياكم إن شاء الله
Insha-Allah	إن شاء الله
Masha-Allah	ما شاء الله
Alhamdulillah	الحمدُ لله
Yarhamakallah	يرحمكم الله

Would you like to sit with the Prophet ﷺ on the Day of Judgment and be close to him?

You can do that if you practice the best Islamic manners.

WORDS OF WISDOM

(Hadeeth Shareef)

حديث شريف

Narrated By Ahmed

عن جابر بن عبدالله رضي الله عنه: قال رسول الله ﷺ :

"إن من أحبكم إلي وأقربكم مِني مجلساً يوم القِيامة أحاسنكم أخلاقاً".

TRANSLITERATION

Inna mun ahabbakum ilai wa aqrabakum minni majlissan yawma alqiyamah ahasinakum akhlaqan.

TRANSLATION

The Prophet ﷺ said: "Should I tell you who among you are the most beloved to me and the closest to me on the Day of Judgment? Those of you who have the best manners."

How can I have the best manners?

One easy way of having good manners is to use the words and expressions that the Prophet ﷺ and his friends used. In other words, following the Sunnah of Rasoolullah ﷺ. It is always better to do things that Rasoolullah ﷺ did because he did the best things. We win great rewards and hasanat when we follow the Sunnah of the Prophet ﷺ.

Let us learn some of these words and their meanings:

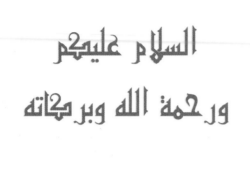

السلام عليكم
ورحمة الله وبركاته

healthy
h a b i t

Do not wait
for others to
greet you.
You start.

1. When we meet we say:

السلام عليكم ورحمة الله وبركاته

Assalamu alaykum
Warahmatullahi Wabarakatuh

It means "May the peace, mercy, and blessings of Allah be upon you."

This expression is used to greet people. Once the Prophet was sitting when a man came and said "Assalamu alaykum." The Prophet ﷺ said "Ten." Another man came and said "Assalamu alaykum wa Rahmatullah." The Prophet said "Twenty." A third man came and said "Assalamu alaykum wa Rahmatullahi Wa Barakatuh." The Prophet said "Thirty." What the Prophet meant was that the first man earned ten hasanat, the second man earned twenty hasanat, and the third man earned thirty hasanat. So you can earn many hasanat just by saying: "Assalamu alaykum Warahmatullahi Wabarakatuh."

بسم الله الرحمن الرحيم

2. Whenever we begin something we say:

بسم الله الرحمن الرحيم

Bismillahi-rrahmani-rraheem

It means "In the Name of Allah, the Most Compassionate, the Most Merciful."

We do not use this expression only before eating. We should also say it before reading, writing, sleeping, getting up, getting dressed, taking a test, reading Qur'an, and at the beginning of almost everything we do!

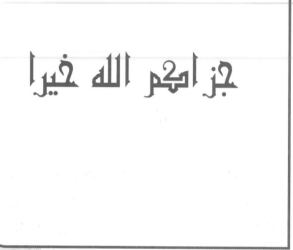

جزاكم الله خيراً

3. When we thank someone, we say:

جزاكم الله خيراً

"Jazakum Allah Khayran"

It means "May Allah give you good rewards."

This expression is used when you want to thank someone. It is also used when someone says something nice to you.

Sarah once thanked her mom for cooking her favorite dinner. She said, "Mom, Jazakillahu Khayran."
When we use this expression, we are making a du'aa' for that person.

What should be your answer when someone says "Jazakum Allah Khayran" to you?

When we are thanked, we respond:

"Wa Iyyakum, ~~Insha-Allah~~ Ameen"

It means, "The same to you, ~~Insha-Allah~~ Ameen".

إن شاء الله

4. When we plan to do something, we say:

إن شاء الله

"Insha-Allah"

It means "If Allah is wills."

We know that things only happen if Allah wants them to. So we say Insha-Allah. What Allah wants to happen will happen, and what Allah does not want to happen will never be.

Example:

- Insha-Allah my family and I are going to Hajj next year.

- Insha-Allah I'm going to study hard for my next test.

5. When we like something, we say:

ما شاء الله

"Masha-Allah"

It means "Whatever Allah wills."

Instead of saying "wow," we should say "Masha-Allah."

Example:

- Masha-Allah, you have a nice home.
- Masha-Allah, you have a beautiful dress.

6. When someone buys something new, for example new clothes or a new bike, you say:

مُـبارك

"Mubarak"

then he or she should reply:

بارَك الله فيك

" Barak Allah feek "

This is of course better than only saying congratulations.

7. When we thank Allah, we say: الحمد لله "Alhamdulillah."
It means "Praise be to Allah." We use this expression to show gratitude to Allah for all of the blessings and gifts He has given us.

There are many times when we can use "Alhamdulillah"
1. When someone asks us how we are doing, instead of saying "fine," we should answer with "Alhamdulillah."
2. Whenever we finish eating or drinking, we should say "Alhamdulillah."
3. When we sneeze, we should say "Alhamdulillah."
4. Whenever we remember one of Allah's many blessings, we should say "Alhamdulillah."

What are some of Allah's blessings and gifts to us?
Alhamdulillah for my loving family.
Alhamdulillah for my good health.
Alhamdulillah for sending me prophets and Books.
Alhamdulillah for the refreshing rain.

الحمد لله

Allah is Perfect in all ways

Alhamdulillah for hot showers. Can you think of some more blessings of Allah? Write them and share them with the class.

5. When you sneeze, you should say الحمد لله Al-hamdulillah. If someone hears you saying that, he or she should say to you " يرحمك الله Yarhamuk Allah", Then you reply " يهديكم الله ويصلح بالكم Yahdeekumu-llahu wa Yuslihu balakum."

WORDS OF WISDOM
Hadeeth Shareef

حديث شريف

Narrated By Ahmed

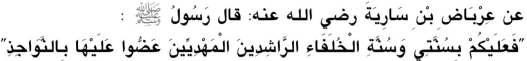

عن عِرْبَاضِ بْنِ سَارِيَةَ رضي الله عنه: قال رَسُولُ ﷺ :
"فَعَلَيْكُمْ بِسُنَّتِي وَسُنَّةِ الْخُلَفَاءِ الرَّاشِدِينَ الْمَهْدِيِّينَ عَضُّوا عَلَيْهَا بِالنَّوَاجِذِ"

TRANSLITERATION

Fa-alaykum bisunnati wa sunnat-ilkhulafaa' irrashdeen
al-mahdiyyeena wa 'odhoo 'alayha binnawajith.

MEANING TRANSLATION

Irbad Ibn Sariya رضي الله عنه reported that Rasoolullah ﷺ said:
"Follow my Sunnah and that of the guided khulafaa' after
me. Stick to it strongly like grabbing it with your teeth."

healthy
h a b i t

Always do things
according to the
Sunnah of the
Prophet.

Think Critically:

❶ Why is using Islamic expressions better than saying ordinary ones?

❷ What should you do when you meet someone who is not a Muslim? Do you use Islamic expressions or ordinary ones? Why?

Study Questions

❶ Why is it important to use Islamic expressions?

❷ What should Muslims say when they greet each other? What does this mean?

❸ What should Muslims say when they start doing something good? What does this mean?

❹ What should Muslims say when they thank each other? What does this mean?

❺ What should Muslims say when they are asked about their health? What does this mean?

❻ What should Muslims say when they congratulate each other? What does this mean?

❼ What should Muslims say when they sneeze? What does this mean?